A Practical Guide to

The Early Years Foundation Stage

Miranda Walker

Nelson Thornes

Published in 2012 by:
Nelson Thornes Ltd
Delta Place
27 Bath Road
CHELTENHAM
GL53 7TH
United Kingdom

12 13 14 15 16 / 10 9 8 7 6 5 4 3 2 1

A catalogue record for this book is available from the British Library

ISBN 978 1 4085 1539 6

Cover photograph: Comstock Images/Getty
Page make-up by Fakenham Prepress Solutions, Fakenham, Norfolk
Printed and bound in Spain by GraphyCems

Contents

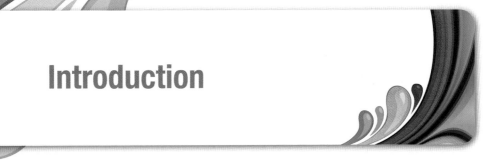

Introduction

This book is a practical guide to the revised Early Years Foundation Stage (EYFS), which became statutory for early years providers in September 2012. With an accessible and informative approach, it's suitable for both experienced practitioners and early years students.

The book introduces the revised framework in terms of structure, overarching principles and the changes made by the 2012 reforms. There's also advice on using the non-statutory Development Matters guidance.

Each of the areas of learning and development within the EYFS is explored and activity ideas to promote each individual early learning goal are included for the birth to 60-month age range.

There's a guide to planning, observation and assessment – including the progress check at age 2 – and finally, there's a guide to safeguarding and welfare requirements, and Ofsted inspections. You can access free, up-to-date information about assessment, including the EYFS profile, by registering at www.planetvocational.co.uk.

How to use this book

It is intended that you read this book alongside the Statutory Framework for the Early Years Foundation Stage and the non-statutory Development Matters guidance. You can download these free of charge from the Foundation Years website. Visit www.foundationyears.org.uk, select 'EYFS' from the menu across the top of the screen and follow the links.

Don't forget

This feature appears throughout the book. It provides interesting and useful facts, and draws attention to key points to enhance your knowledge and promote best practice.

! Don't forget

Ask Miranda!

Your expert author, Miranda Walker, answers all the questions you may have as you progress through the book and helps you on the road to success within the Early Years Foundation Stage.

The following features appear in Part 3 of the book only:

Early learning goal

The early learning goals (ELGs) for each area of learning are given in full and tackled one at a time. Suggested activities are provided that support achievement of the ELGs.

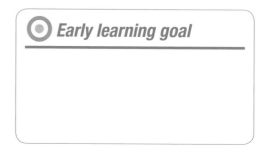

Activity idea

Activity ideas for suggested activities are given for each age range, as specified. Age ranges match the Development Matters guidance. New activities are introduced alongside the important early years staples. Extension ideas are provided at the end of some activities to build on the activity and develop it further.

Activity in focus

For each ELG, a more detailed 'activity in focus', expressed as a step-by-step guide, is provided for one of the age ranges. Extension ideas are provided at the end of some activities to build on the activity and develop it further.

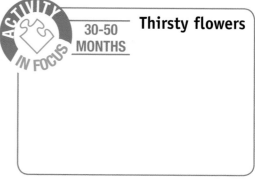

Development matters!

Some Development Matters features, that link to the Development Matters guidance, are provided.

A unique child

Excerpts from child observations show some of the learning that children may exhibit and that you may see during a specific activity.

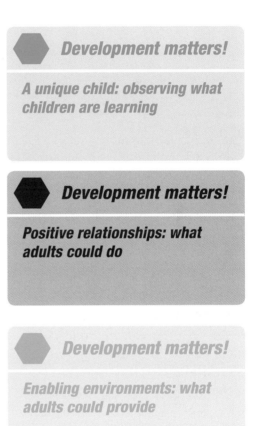

Development matters!

A unique child: observing what children are learning

Positive relationships

Through mini 'case studies', this feature demonstrates practical examples of things you can do to support children's learning and development.

Development matters!

Positive relationships: what adults could do

Enabling environments

This feature focuses on what you, as a practitioner, can provide to support children's learning and development. It includes details of suitable resources to support learning and development, and tips on setting up activities and resources.

Development matters!

Enabling environments: what adults could provide

Planet Vocational

To accompany this book, you will find FREE planning documents and additional information on the Planet Vocational website. Here you will  be kept completely up-to-date with all things related to the EYFS. You will also receive exclusive childcare news and industry updates.

For access, register at www.planetvocational.co.uk

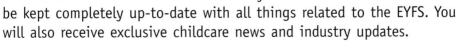

1 Guide to the Statutory Framework for the EYFS

Introduction

The Early Years Foundation Stage (EYFS) framework was first introduced in 2008.

In 2010, the Children's Minister asked Dame Clare Tickell – the Chief Executive of Action for Children – to carry out an independent review of the EYFS framework. An important part of Tickell's task was to consider how the EYFS framework could be more focused on supporting children's early learning and less bureaucratic (by cutting back on paperwork, for example). You can read more about the Tickell Review, including how it was conducted, on pages 14–15.

In March 2011, the Tickell Review recommended a number of changes. The Government responded by significantly reforming the 2008 version of the EYFS framework.

The new, revised framework, covered in this book, became mandatory for all early years providers in England on 1 September 2012. This means it must be delivered by maintained schools, non-maintained schools, independent schools and all providers on the Early Years Register – this includes pre-schools, nurseries, children's centres and childminders.

In Part 1 of the book you'll be introduced to:

- the overarching principles of the new EYFS framework
- an overview of the Tickell Review
- the key changes that have been made to the framework in the reform.

> **❗ Don't forget**
>
> -
>
> The full name of the official document which sets out the revised EYFS framework is the Statutory Framework for the Early Years Foundation Stage. We generally refer to this as the EYFS framework for short.

Figure 1.1 The revised EYFS framework became mandatory for all early years settings in September 2012

The overarching principles of the revised EYFS

The Statutory Framework for the Early Years Foundation Stage document tells us that:

1. Every child deserves the best possible start in life and the support that enables them to fulfil their potential. Children develop quickly in the early years and a child's experiences between birth and age 5 have a major impact on their future life chances. A secure, safe and

happy childhood is important in its own right. Good parenting and high quality early learning together provide the foundation children need to make the most of their abilities and talents as they grow up.

2. The Early Years Foundation Stage sets the standards that all early years providers must meet to ensure that children learn and develop well and are kept healthy and safe. It promotes teaching and learning to ensure children's 'school readiness' and gives children the broad range of knowledge and skills that provide the right foundation for good future progress through school and life.

Ask Miranda!

Q: What does the term 'school readiness' mean?

A: There's been some debate about the phrase 'school readiness', which is used in the EYFS framework. There's no doubt that young children who experience a high standard of teaching and learning are more likely to fare well at school. This is because the learning and development experienced in the early years underpins the learning and development achieved later.

However, there is some concern that the term 'school readiness' gives the impression that young children in early years settings should be expected to behave and learn in formal ways, so they are used to doing things such as sitting still and being quiet for quite long periods (in readiness for activities such as school assemblies) by the time they start school. In reality, these things are inappropriate for younger children, who have different learning and development needs to older children. It's important to understand that **being ready for school does not mean already doing the things expected of older children.**

A good knowledge of child development will help you to prepare young children for school by ensuring that the teaching and learning they experience is right for them **now**. This will give them the best foundation for fulfilling their potential in the future.

You'll learn more about how to use the Development Matters in the Early Years Foundation Stage (EYFS) guidance to support children's learning and development appropriately during the EYFS in Part 2 of this book.

3. The EYFS framework seeks to provide:

    - quality and consistency in all early years settings, so that every child makes good progress and no child gets left behind

    - a secure foundation through learning and development opportunities which are planned around the needs and interests of each individual child, and are assessed and reviewed regularly

    - partnership working between practitioners and with parents and/ or carers

    - equality of opportunity and anti-discriminatory practice, ensuring that every child is included and supported.

Figure 1.2 Emphasis is placed on partnership working between practitioners and parents/carers in the revised framework

4. The EYFS framework specifies requirements for learning and development, and for safeguarding children and promoting their welfare. The learning and development requirements cover:

    - the areas of learning and development which must shape activities and experiences (educational programmes) for children in all early years settings

Guide to the Statutory Framework for the EYFS

- the early learning goals that providers must help children work towards (the knowledge, skills and understanding children should have at the end of the academic year in which they turn 5)

- assessment arrangements for measuring children's progress (and the requirements for reporting this to parents and/or carers).

We'll look at how each of these requirements fits into the overall structure of the EYFS framework on pages 21–31. We'll then explore the areas of learning and development in detail in Part 3 of this book, and we'll look at assessment in detail in Part 4.

5. The safeguarding and welfare requirements cover the steps that providers must take to keep children safe and promote their welfare.

We'll look at these safeguarding and welfare requirements in detail in Part 5 of this book.

Overarching principles

6. The EYFS framework states that *four* guiding principles should shape practice in early years settings. These are:

- every child is a unique child, who is constantly learning and can be resilient, capable, confident and self-assured

- children learn to be strong and independent through positive relationships

- children learn and develop well in enabling environments, in which their experiences respond to their individual needs, and there is a strong partnership between practitioners and parents and/or carers

- children develop and learn in different ways and at different rates. The EYFS framework covers the education and care of all children in early years provision, including children with special educational needs and disabilities.

❗ *Don't forget*

You'll learn more about the four guiding principles and how to promote them through EYFS provision when we look at how to use the Development Matters in the Early Years Foundation Stage (EYFS) guidance in Part 2 of this book. The guidance is closely linked to the overarching principles.

The Tickell Review

As mentioned in the introduction, Dame Clare Tickell carried out an independent review of the 2008 EYFS framework. The review covered four main areas:

1. **Scope of regulation** – whether there should be one single framework for all early years providers.

2. **Learning and development** – looking at the latest evidence about children's development and what is needed to give them the best start at school.

3. **Assessment** – whether young children's development should be formally assessed at a certain age, and what this should cover.

4. **Welfare** – the minimum standards to keep children safe and support their healthy development.

Department for Education website: Tickell-Review – background

The review was conducted using a number of research methods:

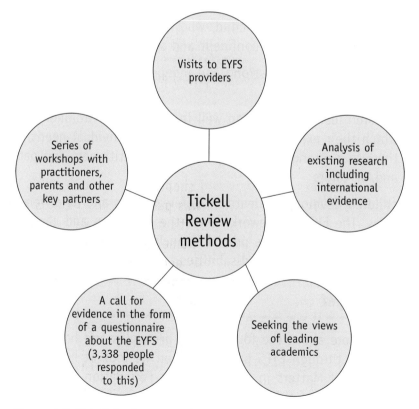

Figure 1.3 Tickell Review research methods

Guide to the Statutory Framework for the EYFS

Tickell's recommendations

Once the research phase was completed, Tickell analysed the results and made a number of recommendations on how the EYFS could be improved. The recommendations were published in her final report in March 2011. The Government went on to significantly reform the EYFS framework in response to the recommendations.

According to the 'Reforms to the 2012 EYFS Framework' document published by the Department for Education, the reforms that were made are intended to:

- reduce paperwork and bureaucracy

- strengthen partnerships between parents and professionals

- focus on the three prime areas of learning most essential for children's readiness for future learning and healthy development

- simplify assessment at age 5

- provide for early intervention where necessary, through the introduction of a progress check at age 2.

> **❗ Don't forget**
> --
> The revised framework became mandatory for early years providers on 1 September 2012.

Key changes made in the 2012 EYFS reform

If you are new to early years, you will simply learn about the revised version of the EYFS framework, which was published in 2012. As the following Ask Miranda! question shows, it's normal to feel a little apprehensive about understanding the framework at first, but there is no need to worry about it unduly – this book will support you along the way. Read the question and answer on page 16, then turn to page 21 to start learning about the revised framework.

However, if you have previously been involved in delivering the 2008 version of the EYFS framework (or have learned about it, perhaps at college), it's helpful to have an overview of the key differences between the 2008 version and the revised 2012 version. This is provided on pages 16–21, so read on!

Ask Miranda!

Q: I'm new to early years and I'm worried about taking in so much information and doing everything right. What's the best way to cope?

A: It's true that there's quite a lot of information to absorb, but there's plenty of advice and help available to you in this book and beyond, and there are some excellent resources available too. I'll be pointing you towards them throughout. No one expects you to know everything right away, so take your time and work through the book at your own pace. I introduce the structure of the revised EYFS framework on pages 21–31. Understanding this is the key to becoming familiar with a) how the EYFS is delivered by practitioners, and b) the language and terminology used.

You'll probably find it helpful to return to pages 21–31 to refresh your memory now and then as you work through other parts of the book – it is your first port of call if you feel a little confused about how the EYFS framework works at any stage.

Remember that your tutors, your colleagues and your placement supervisors are a good source of advice, help and experience. They have been in your shoes – they were once new to early years too!

Reforms to the learning and development requirements

As stated in the 'Reforms to the 2012 EYFS Framework' document published by the Department for Education, the key reforms made to the learning and development requirements fall into six categories:

1. **Areas of learning and development:** these now consist of three prime areas and four specific areas. Previously there were six areas of learning and development. The three prime areas cover the knowledge and skills which are the foundations for children's school readiness and future progress. These are applied and reinforced by the four specific areas. Where they have close links with National Curriculum subject areas – particularly literacy and maths – they form an appropriate baseline for the National Curriculum (or, in other words, they lay an effective foundation for the learning that children will do at school).

2. **Early learning goals and assessment:** instead of 69 goals, there are now just 17. Instead of the current set of judgements against 117 scale-points, practitioners will assess children's progress against the 17 early learning goals. For each goal, practitioners determine whether children are meeting expected levels, are exceeding them, or are below the expected level ('emerging'). Providers are required to share the report on each child, along with a brief report on the characteristics of learning, with the Year 1 teacher.

3. **Progress check at age 2:** the revised EYFS framework has introduced a requirement for providers to review children's progress when a child is aged between 2 and 3. A short written summary must be provided to parents or carers, highlighting achievements and areas in which extra support might be needed, and describing how the provider will address any issues.

4. **Play and teaching:** it has been made clearer that providers are responsible for ongoing judgements about the balance between play and teaching, between activities led by children and activities led or guided by adults.

5. **English as an additional language:** the relevant requirements give clearer focus on the reasonable steps providers must take, including the assessment of children's skills in English.

6. **Wraparound and holiday care:** The framework now makes clear that the EYFS requirements do not need to be delivered in full when children spend limited amounts of time in a setting.

Ask Miranda!

Q: I'm used to the 2008 version of the EYFS framework. I had a lot of training on it and now it seems it will all go to waste. Is it going to be hard to get my head around the revised framework? It was bad enough doing that in 2008!

A: Your previous training and knowledge won't go to waste. Children haven't changed, and you'll continue to do plenty of things in the same way as before. As you become more familiar with the revised framework, you'll find a lot of things haven't changed significantly, if at all.

Of course, there are some changes to get used to. The good news is that, on the whole, the majority of the changes have been widely regarded as positive improvements by early years professionals – although there are always a few bones of contention. It's likely that the simplification of the framework achieved in the reform will have some practitioners sighing with relief and looking forward to new working methods with less bureaucracy and paperwork.

Figure 1.4 The revised framework aims to reduce paperwork

Reforms to the welfare requirements

To emphasise the importance of safeguarding children, the welfare requirements of the 2008 EYFS framework have been renamed the *safeguarding and welfare requirements*. We'll look at these in detail in Part 5 of the book, but the key reforms, as stated in the 'Reforms to the 2012 EYFS Framework' published by the Department for Education, are highlighted here.

- **Child protection:** the revised EYFS framework includes examples of adults' behaviour which might be signs of abuse and neglect. If they become aware of any such signs, staff should respond appropriately in order to safeguard children.

- The EYFS framework now requires that safeguarding policies and procedures cover the use of mobile phones and cameras in the setting.

- **Suitable people:** the requirements for providers to check the suitability of managers have been simplified. From September 2012, providers are responsible for obtaining criminal record disclosures on managers. Prior to this, Ofsted obtained these disclosures.

- **Staff qualifications, training, support and skills:** a requirement has been introduced in relation to staff supervision. Providers must give staff opportunities for coaching and training, mutual support, teamwork and continuous improvement; also confidential discussion of sensitive issues.

- The requirement for childminders to complete training in the EYFS has been strengthened. Childminders will be required to complete the training before they register with Ofsted.

- **Staff:child ratios:** there is a clarification of the circumstances in which there may be exceptions to the staff:child ratios for childminders caring for children of mixed ages.

- **Safety and suitability of premises, environment and equipment:** the requirements in relation to risk assessment have been adjusted to clarify that it is up to providers to judge whether a risk assessment needs to be recorded in writing.

▶

baby room of a day nursery there must be one member of staff for every three babies under the age of 2. This is expressed as a ratio of 1:3. (There are additional requirements about the qualifications of staff – you'll learn more in Part 5 of this book.)

Ask Miranda!

Q: So can I just stop doing risk assessments in writing if I don't think they're necessary?

A: It's not quite that simple in practice. You still need to work in line with the individual policies and procedures of your setting. However, many settings will be looking closely at their staff guidelines on risk assessment as a result of this reform, as the new requirement has the potential to reduce unnecessary bureaucracy (official procedure and admin).

It's important to ensure that you fully understand any changes your setting makes to risk assessment guidelines, so you are confident about a) when a written risk assessment is still necessary, and b) the risk assessment process you must still run through mentally/verbally to ensure the safety and suitability of the premises, environment and equipment. It's good practice for settings to consult staff on a policy review – this will enable a thorough discussion about the implications of changing the way risk assessment is undertaken by staff within the setting.

❗ Don't forget

When making changes to risk assessment policies and procedures, settings must ensure that they continue to meet all clauses of their current insurance policies.

Guide to the Statutory Framework for the EYFS

The structure of the revised EYFS framework

Accessing the framework

In the past, settings were sent a hard copy of the EYFS framework and a range of supporting resources, both in hard copy and on CD, and duplicate information was available on the internet. This has changed.

The revised framework and other supporting resources from the Department of Education are now *only* provided on a dedicated website, www.foundationyears.org.uk. Settings and/or practitioners *must* go online to print out copies for themselves, or to refer to the information on screen. However, some organisations (such as the National Day Nurseries Association – NDNA) are selling published copies of the EYFS framework and the Development Matters guidance for those who prefer not to print them off themselves. (This information is correct at the time of writing. You'll learn about the Development Matters guidance in Part 2 of this book.)

To access the full revised EYFS framework and supporting material, visit www.foundationyears.org.uk. Select 'EYFS' from the menu across the top of the screen and follow the links.

Figure 1.5 Access EYFS guidance online

> **❗ Don't forget**
> -
>
> All practitioners need to have access to the full revised EYFS framework and supporting guidance and resources, including the Development Matters guidance. It's a good idea to have these with you for reference as you work through this book.

Staying up to date

While you're on the Foundation Years website, browse the additional information and advice on offer. You'll see that there's an EYFS news section and also an online forum that enables practitioners to share their views. Sign up for the newsletter, which will be delivered to your email inbox. It will help you to stay up to date with developments in the EYFS and it will make you aware of any additional supporting materials or resources that become available – this is important for your ongoing professional practice and development. It will also give you confidence as you move forward with the delivery of the revised EYFS framework. Regularly reading industry magazines and journals (such as *Nursery World*) is also recommended.

The sections of the framework

The EYFS framework is made up of three main sections. A brief overview is given here – you'll learn much more about each section as you work through this book:

Section 1 – The learning and development requirements

This section of the framework tells us what early years providers must do, working in partnership with parents and/or carers, to promote the learning and development of all children in their care.

There are seven areas of learning and development that must shape educational programmes in early years settings. All areas of learning and development are important and inter-connected. Three areas are particularly crucial for igniting children's curiosity and enthusiasm for learning, and for building their capacity to learn, form relationships and thrive. These three areas, known as the prime areas of learning and development, are:

- communication and language

- physical development
- personal, social and emotional development.

Providers must also support children in four specific areas of learning and development, through which the three prime areas are strengthened and applied. The specific areas are:

- literacy
- mathematics
- understanding the world
- expressive arts and design.

Educational programmes must involve activities and experiences for children as follows (we will explore this in much greater depth in Part 3 of this book):

- **Communication and language development** involves giving children opportunities to experience a rich language environment, to develop their confidence and skills in expressing themselves, and to speak and listen in a range of situations.

- **Physical development** involves providing opportunities for young children to be active and interactive, and to develop their coordination, control and movement. Children must also be helped to understand the importance of physical activity, and to make healthy choices in relation to food.

- **Personal, social and emotional development** involves helping children to develop a positive sense of themselves, and others; to form positive relationships and develop respect for others; to develop social skills and learn how to manage their feelings; to understand appropriate behaviour in groups; and to have confidence in their own abilities.

- **Literacy development** involves encouraging children to link sounds and letters, and to begin to read and write. Children must be given access to a wide range of reading materials (books, poems and other written materials) to ignite their interest.

- **Mathematics** involves providing children with opportunities to develop and improve their skills in counting, understanding and using numbers, calculating simple addition and subtraction problems; and describing shapes, spaces, and measures.

- **Understanding the world** involves guiding children to make sense of their physical world and their community through opportunities to explore, observe and find out about people, places, technology and the environment.

- **Expressive arts and design** involves enabling children to explore and play with a wide range of media and materials. It also involves providing opportunities and encouragement for children to share their thoughts, ideas and feelings through a variety of activities in art, music, movement, dance, role play, and design and technology.

Practitioners must consider the individual needs, interests and stage of development of each child in their care, and must use this information to plan a challenging and enjoyable experience for them in all of the areas of learning and development.

Practitioners working with the youngest children are expected to focus strongly on the three prime areas, which are the basis for successful learning in the other four specific areas.

Figure 1.6 Practitioners working with the youngest children are expected to focus strongly on the three prime areas

Guide to the Statutory Framework for the EYFS

The three prime areas reflect the key skills and capacities all children need to develop and learn effectively. It is expected that the balance will shift towards a more equal focus on all areas of learning as children grow in confidence and ability within the three prime areas.

If a child's progress gives cause for concern

According to Section 1 of the framework, throughout the early years, if a child's progress in any prime area gives cause for concern, practitioners must discuss this with the child's parents and/or carers and agree how to support the child. Practitioners must consider whether a child may have a special educational need or disability which requires specialist support. They should link with, and help families to access, relevant services from other agencies, as appropriate.

Planning and guiding children's activities

The EYFS framework states that, in planning and guiding children's activities, practitioners must reflect on the different ways that children learn, and reflect these in their practice. Three characteristics of effective teaching and learning are:

- **playing and exploring:** children investigate and experience things, and 'have a go'

- **active learning:** children concentrate and keep on trying if they encounter difficulties, and enjoy achievements

- **creating and thinking critically:** children have and develop their own ideas, make links between ideas, and develop strategies for doing things.

The early learning goals

For each area of learning, the EYFS framework sets out early learning goals. These set out the level of progress children should be expected to have attained by the end of the EYFS. To put it another way, the purpose of the educational programmes provided by practitioners is to enable children to reach the early learning goals by the end of the EYFS. The early learning goals for each area of learning are expressed in full in Part 3 of this book.

Section 2 – Assessment

This section of the EYFS framework tells us that assessment plays an important part in helping parents, carers and practitioners to recognise children's progress, understand their needs, and to plan activities and support. Ongoing assessment (also known as formative assessment) is an integral part of the learning and development process. It involves practitioners observing children to understand their level of achievement, interests and learning styles, and to then shape learning experiences for each child reflecting those observations. In their interactions with children, practitioners should respond to:

- their own day-to-day observations about children's progress

- observations that parents and carers share.

Figure 1.7 Ongoing assessment is an integral part of the learning and development process

Parents and/or carers should be kept up to date with their child's progress and development. Practitioners should address any learning and development needs identified in partnership with parents and/or carers, and any relevant professionals.

(We'll look at observation and assessment in detail in Part 4 of this book.)

Progress check at age 2

The EYFS framework states that when a child is aged between 2 and 3, practitioners must review their progress, and provide parents and/or carers with a short written summary of their child's development in the prime areas. This progress check must:

- identify the child's strengths

- identify any areas where the child's progress is less than expected.

If there are significant emerging concerns, or an identified special educational need or disability, practitioners should develop a targeted plan to support the child's future learning and development involving other professionals (for example, the provider's Special Educational Needs Coordinator – SENCO), as appropriate.

Practitioners must discuss with parents and/or carers how the summary of their child's development can be used to support learning at home.

❗ Don't forget

- -

Practitioners should encourage parents and/or carers to share information from the progress check with other relevant professionals, including their health visitor and/or a teacher.

Ask Miranda!

Q: Is it up to me when I do the progress check, as long as it's between the age of 2 and 3?

A: The EYFS framework tells us that practitioners must agree with parents and/or carers when the most useful point to provide a summary will be. It should be provided in time to inform the

Healthy Child Programme health and development review at age 2 whenever possible. (This is when health visitors gather information on a child's health and development, enabling them to identify any developmental delay and any particular support from which they think the child/family might benefit.)

The Early Years Foundation Stage profile

The EYFS profile is an assessment document which must be completed for every child in the final term of the year in which they reach the age of five (the end of the EYFS). This involves assessing the child's level of development against the early learning goals. The EYFS framework states that practitioners must indicate whether children are meeting expected levels of development, or if they are exceeding expected levels, or not yet reaching expected levels ('emerging').

The EYFS profile provides parents and carers, practitioners and teachers with a well-rounded picture of:

- a child's knowledge, understanding and abilities
- their progress against expected levels
- their readiness for Year 1 of school.

The profile must reflect:

- ongoing observation
- all relevant records held by the setting about the child
- discussions with parents and carers, and any other relevant adults.

Information to be provided to the local authority

Under the requirements of the EYFS framework, early years providers must report EYFS profile results to local authorities, upon request. Local authorities are under a duty to return this data to the relevant Government department.

Section 3 – The safeguarding and welfare requirements

This section of the EYFS framework tells us that children learn best when:

- they are healthy
- they are safe and secure

- their individual needs are met
- they have positive relationships with the adults caring for them.

The safeguarding and welfare requirements of the EYFS framework are designed to 'help providers create high quality settings which are welcoming, safe and stimulating, and where children are able to enjoy learning and grow in confidence. Providers must take all necessary steps to keep children safe and well.' The requirements explain what early years providers must do to:

- safeguard children
- ensure the suitability of adults who have contact with children
- promote good health
- manage behaviour
- maintain records, policies and procedures.

We'll look at the safeguarding and welfare requirements in each of the above areas in detail in Part 5 of this book.

Figure 1.8 Providers must take all necessary steps to keep children safe and well

Ofsted

Ofsted is the official body which has responsibility for the EYFS framework. It's Ofsted's job to carry out inspections of all early years settings and to report on the quality and standards of the provision. Ofsted publishes inspection reports at www.ofsted.gov.uk.

Should an Ofsted inspector find that an EYFS provider is failing to meet an EYFS requirement, they may issue the setting with a notice to improve and/or may issue a welfare requirements notice (if the failure relates to Section 3 of the framework).

We'll look at Ofsted in more detail in Part 5 of this book.

❗ Don't forget

It is an offence for a provider to fail to comply with a welfare requirements notice. Ultimately, a provider who fails to comply may have their provision closed down by Ofsted.

Ask Miranda!

Q: What should I do with all my resources for the old EYFS framework – throw them out?

A: No, hold on to them! There's a lot of good information in them. The trick is to work out which parts to continue using and which are no longer relevant. It's a good idea for colleagues to bring all their old resources and documents along to a meeting, and to work out together what can still be used. It's worth remembering that websites that featured favourite resources for the 2008 EYFS framework may no longer be live, but many of the resources themselves still exist in online archives. (An internet search will usually track them down.)

Having said that, it's important to explore the new resources and specific guidance available to support the revised EYFS framework too – so make sure you don't cling too much to those familiar 'safe' ones – it could prevent your practice from developing.

❗ Don't forget

If you're leaving resources or documents from the old EYFS framework on the shelf in your setting, it's well worth marking on them clearly that they've been archived and that they do not refer to the current framework. This is important, as newer practitioners and learners can otherwise become understandably confused when browsing the bookshelf or, worse still, when choosing resources to help them with their learning or assignments!

2 Guide to Development Matters in the EYFS

The Development Matters in the Early Years Foundation Stage (EYFS) guidance

The Development Matters in the Early Years Foundation Stage (EYFS) guidance has been produced by Early Education to support you in implementing the statutory requirements of the revised EYFS framework. It consists of detailed development charts covering:

- what you can expect to observe children learning from birth to 5 years

- what you can do to support this learning through your interactions with children and the environment you provide.

Unlike the EYFS framework, the Development Matters guidance is non-statutory.

Ask Miranda!

Q: What does 'non-statutory' mean?

A: It means 'not mandatory'. Or, in other words, early years providers are not legally required to use Development Matters when delivering the EYFS. But it's an excellent, helpful resource, as you'll read below, so it's a good idea to make use of it.

Accessing the guidance

Excerpts from the Development Matters guidance are reproduced here. However, it is a long document and ideally you should have a full copy to refer to as you read this part of the book. You can download the Development Matters guidance from the EYFS section of the Foundation Years website.

> **❗ Don't forget**
> --
>
> The Foundation Years website address is www.foundationyears.org.uk.
> If you prefer not to print the Development Matters guidance yourself
> but would still like a hard copy (there are many coloured pages
> and photos to print off), you can buy a printed version from Early
> Education online – visit www.early-education.org.uk and follow the
> links. You should also be able to borrow a copy from your workplace
> or placement setting.

The purpose of the guidance

The Development Matters guidance shows how the four themes of the
EYFS framework and the principles that inform them work together to
support babies and children. This is important because the principles
must shape practice in every early years setting.

The opening statement of the guidance expands on its purpose by telling
us that:

'Children develop quickly in the early years, and practitioners aim to
do all they can to help children have the best possible start in life.
Children have a right, spelled out in the United Nations Convention on
the Rights of the Child, to provision which enables them to develop
their personalities, talents and abilities irrespective of ethnicity, culture,
religion, home language, family background, learning difficulties,
disabilities or gender. This guidance helps adults to understand and
support each individual child's development pathway.'

> **❗ Don't forget**
> --
>
> You were introduced to the guiding principles of the EYFS framework
> in Part 1 of this book – you may like to turn back to page 13 and
> recap the information before reading on. You will need to be familiar
> with what is meant by the following terms:
> * unique child
> * positive relationships
> * enabling environments

▶

- children developing and learning in different ways and at different rates
- the characteristics of effective learning (see next page).

These are used throughout the Development Matters guidance and are explained on pages 35–36.

Figure 2.1 A young child participating in active learning

Guide to Development Matters in the EYFS

The characteristics of effective learning

As you know, the fourth guiding principle of the EYFS framework is that children develop and learn in different ways and at different rates.

There are three associated key characteristics of effective learning which underpin this. These are:

- playing and exploring
- active learning
- creating and thinking critically.

The key characteristics of effective learning are important because they help us to recognise what children are most likely to be doing when they are experiencing high quality learning opportunities. This knowledge helps us to plan the activities and experiences that we offer children in our settings. It's good practice to ask yourself how the activities you intend to provide will promote one or more of the key characteristics.

❗ Don't forget

In your overall provision of activities and experiences, you should aim to provide opportunities for children to learn through all three techniques – through playing and exploring, active learning and creating and thinking critically. This gives them a broad learning experience, and it also reflects the fact that different children learn and develop in different ways.

The structure of the Development Matters guidance

The themes and principles of the EYFS framework

Page 2 of the Development Matters guidance (reproduced on page 36) expands on the themes and principles of the EYFS framework. Here we can learn more about:

- what practitioners do to promote the theme of a unique child
- the characteristics of positive relationships established with children by practitioners
- what practitioners do to provide an enabling environment for children

Children are born ready, able and eager to learn. They actively reach out to interact with other people, and in the world around them. Development is not an automatic process, however. It depends on each unique child having opportunities to interact in positive relationships and enabling environments.

The four themes of the EYFS underpin all the guidance. This document - Development Matters - shows how these themes, and the principles that inform them, work together for children in the EYFS.

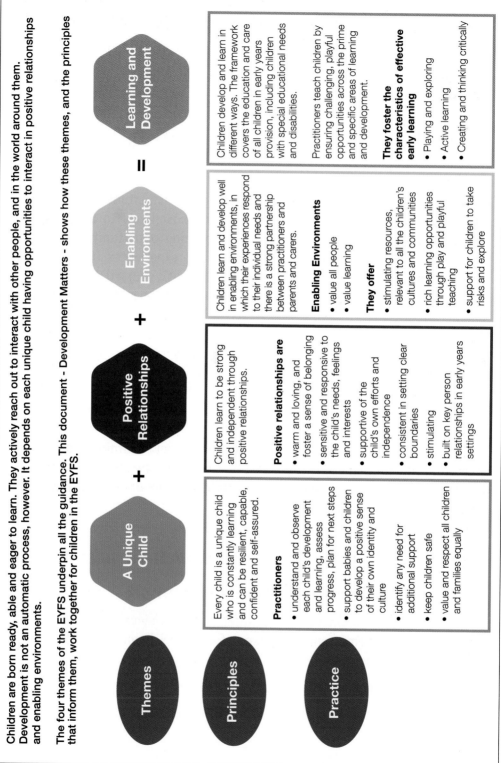

Themes

A Unique Child   +   Positive Relationships   +   Enabling Environments   =   Learning and Development

Principles

Every child is a unique child who is constantly learning and can be resilient, capable, confident and self-assured.

Children learn to be strong and independent through positive relationships.

Children learn and develop well in enabling environments, in which their experiences respond to their individual needs and there is a strong partnership between practitioners and parents and carers.

Children develop and learn in different ways. The framework covers the education and care of all children in early years provision, including children with special educational needs and disabilities.

Practice

Practitioners

- understand and observe each child's development and learning, assess progress, plan for next steps
- support babies and children to develop a positive sense of their own identity and culture
- identify any need for additional support
- keep children safe
- value and respect all children and families equally

Positive relationships are

- warm and loving, and foster a sense of belonging
- sensitive and responsive to the child's needs, feelings and interests
- supportive of the child's own efforts and independence
- consistent in setting clear boundaries
- stimulating
- built on key person relationships in early years settings

Enabling Environments

- value all people
- value learning

They offer

- stimulating resources, relevant to all the children's cultures and communities
- rich learning opportunities through play and playful teaching
- support for children to take risks and explore

Practitioners teach children by ensuring challenging, playful opportunities across the prime and specific areas of learning and development.

They foster the characteristics of effective early learning

- Playing and exploring
- Active learning
- Creating and thinking critically

Figure 2.2 How the themes and principles of the EYFS framework underpin the Development Matters guidance

- what practitioners do to promote children's development and learning, and how all of the above also contributes to the overall learning and development of each child.

Ask Miranda!

Q: The positive relationships column on page 2 of the Development Matters guidance mentions building on 'key person relationships' in the setting. What are 'key person relationships'?

A: It's a requirement of the EYFS framework for each child to have a member of staff designated as their key worker. This person will take a special interest in the welfare of the child, getting to know them and their parents or carers well. This ensures that each child has the opportunity to form a deeper relationship with an adult on a one-to-one basis. Young children need to make this kind of key attachment for their emotional well-being. Most key workers will look after the interests of several key children. They will also have the main responsibility for observing and assessing the development of their key children and liaising with their parents or carers.

Assessment

Page 3 of the Development Matters guidance (reproduced on page 38) gives an overview of how you can use the guidance to help support children's learning and development. We'll explore using the guidance to support observation and assessment in detail in Part 4 of this book.

❗ Don't forget

The Development Matters guidance replaces Appendix 2 of the 2008 EYFS practice guidance.

Using this guidance to support each child's learning and development

Development matters can help practitioners to support children's learning and development, by closely matching what they provide to a child's current needs.

On-going **formative assessment** is at the heart of effective early years practice. Practitioners can:

- Observe children as they act and interact in their play, everyday activities and planned activities, and learn from parents about what the child does at home **(observation)**.

- Consider the examples of development in the columns headed 'Unique Child: observing what children can do' to help identify where the child may be in their own developmental pathway **(assessment)**.

- Consider ways to support the child to strengthen and deepen their current learning and development, reflecting on guidance in columns headed 'Positive Relationships' and 'Enabling Environments' **(planning)**. These columns contain some examples of what practitioners might do to support learning. Practitioners will develop many other approaches in response to the children with whom they work.

- Where appropriate, use the development statements to identify possible areas in which to challenge and extend the child's current learning and development **(planning)**.

This way of teaching is particularly appropriate to support learning in early years settings.

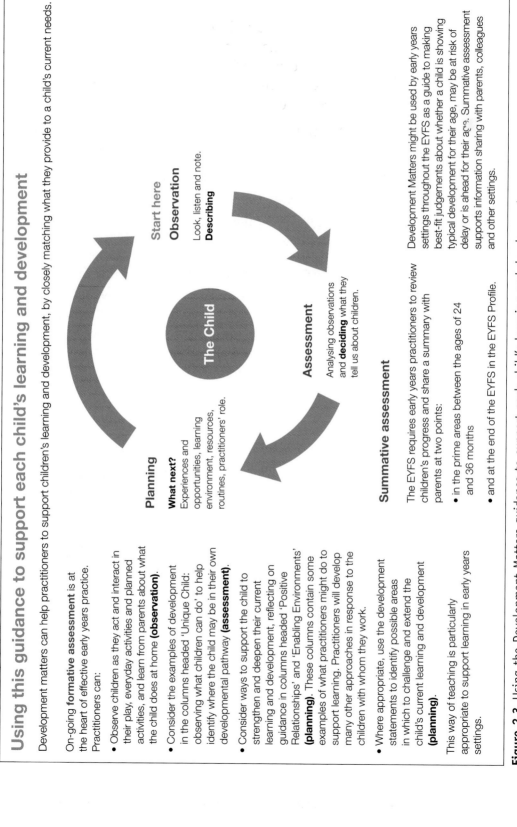

Start here

Observation

Look, listen and note.
Describing

Planning

What next?
Experiences and opportunities, learning environment, resources, routines, practitioners' role.

The Child

Assessment

Analysing observations and **deciding** what they tell us about children.

Summative assessment

The EYFS requires early years practitioners to review children's progress and share a summary with parents at two points:

- in the prime areas between the ages of 24 and 36 months

- and at the end of the EYFS in the EYFS Profile.

Development Matters might be used by early years settings throughout the EYFS as a guide to making best-fit judgements about whether a child is showing typical development for their age, may be at risk of delay or is ahead for their age. Summative assessment supports information sharing with parents, colleagues and other settings.

Figure 2.3 Using the Development Matters guidance to support each child's learning and development

The interconnection of areas of learning

Although we refer to different areas of learning for easy reference, in practice children's learning is not compartmentalised. This means that all areas of learning are connected. For instance, an activity such as planting seeds in the garden with a small group of children might promote learning and development in the following areas:

- **communication and language**: following instructions, answering 'how' and 'why' questions

- **physical development**: using control and coordination of movements, handling gardening equipment

- **personal, social and emotional development**: taking turns with other children, speaking in a group

- **understanding of the world**: knowing about living things and features of the environment.

Page 4 of the Development Matters guidance highlights the connections between the areas of learning. It also shows links between the characteristics of effective learning and the areas of learning, so look out for this in your own copy of the guidance.

Links between the key characteristics of effective learning and the EYFS themes/principles

Pages 6 and 7 of the Development Matters guidance (reproduced on pages 40 and 41) are extremely helpful as they give excellent practical guidance on how you can promote a unique child, positive relationships and enabling environments by utilising effective learning techniques in your work with children.

Each of the key characteristics of effective learning below is broken down into subsections and expanded upon:

- **Playing and exploring** is broken down into:
  - finding out and exploring
  - playing with what they know
  - being willing to 'have a go'.

- **Active learning** is broken down into:
  - being involved and concentrating

Characteristics of Effective Learning

	A Unique Child: observing how a child is learning	Positive Relationships: what adults could do	Enabling Environments: what adults could provide
Playing and Exploring *engagement*	**Finding out and exploring** • Showing curiosity about objects, events and people • Using senses to explore the world around them • Engaging in open-ended activity • Showing particular interests **Playing with what they know** • Pretending objects are things from their experience • Representing their experiences in play • Taking on a role in their play • Acting out experiences with other people **Being willing to 'have a go'** • Initiating activities • Seeking challenge • Showing a 'can do' attitude • Taking a risk, engaging in new experiences, and learning by trial and error	• Play with children. Encourage them to explore, and show your own interest in discovering new things. • Help children as needed to do what they are trying to do, without taking over or directing. • Join in play sensitively, fitting in with children's ideas. • Model pretending an object is something else, and help develop roles and stories. • Encourage children to try new activities and to judge risks for themselves. Be sure to support children's confidence with words and body language. • Pay attention to how children engage in activities -- the challenges faced, the effort, thought, learning and enjoyment. Talk more about the process than products. • Talk about how you and the children get better at things through effort and practice, and what we all can learn when things go wrong.	• Provide stimulating resources which are accessible and open-ended so they can be used, moved and combined in a variety of ways. • Make sure resources are relevant to children's interests. • Arrange flexible indoor and outdoor space and resources where children can explore, build, move and role play. • Help children concentrate by limiting noise, and making spaces visually calm and orderly. • Plan first-hand experiences and challenges appropriate to the development of the children. • Ensure children have uninterrupted time to play and explore.
	A Unique Child: observing how a child is learning	Positive Relationships: what adults could do	Enabling Environments: what adults could provide
Active Learning *motivation*	**Being involved and concentrating** • Maintaining focus on their activity for a period of time • Showing high levels of energy, fascination • Not easily distracted • Paying attention to details **Keeping on trying** • Persisting with activity when challenges occur • Showing a belief that more effort or a different approach will pay off • Bouncing back after difficulties **Enjoying achieving what they set out to do** • Showing satisfaction in meeting their own goals • Being proud of how they accomplished something – not just the end result • Enjoying meeting challenges for their own sake rather than external rewards or praise	• Support children to choose their activities – what they want to do and how they will do it. • Stimulate children's interest through shared attention, and calm over-stimulated children. • Help children to become aware of their own goals, make plans, and to review their own progress and successes. Describe what you see them trying to do, and encourage children to talk about their own processes and successes. • Be specific when you praise, especially noting effort such as how the child concentrates, tries different approaches, persists, solves problems, and has new ideas. • Encourage children to learn together and from each other. • Children develop their own motivations when you give reasons and talk about learning, rather than just directing.	• Children will become more deeply involved when you provide something that is new and unusual for them to explore, especially when it is linked to their interests. • Notice what arouses children's curiosity, looking for signs of deep involvement to identify learning that is intrinsically motivated. • Ensure children have time and freedom to become deeply involved in activities. • Children can maintain focus on things that interest them over a period of time. Help them to keep ideas in mind by talking over photographs of their previous activities. • Keep significant activities out instead of routinely tidying them away. • Make space and time for all children to contribute.

Characteristics of Effective Learning

	A Unique Child: observing how a child is learning	Positive Relationships: what adults could do	Enabling Environments: what adults could provide
Creating and Thinking Critically *thinking*	**Having their own ideas** • Thinking of ideas • Finding ways to solve problems • Finding new ways to do things **Making links** • Making links and noticing patterns in their experience • Making predictions • Testing their ideas • Developing ideas of grouping, sequences, cause and effect **Choosing ways to do things** • Planning, making decisions about how to approach a task, solve a problem and reach a goal • Checking how well their activities are going • Changing strategy as needed • Reviewing how well the approach worked	• Use the language of thinking and learning: *think, know, remember, forget, idea, makes sense, plan, learn, find out, confused, figure out, trying to do.* • Model being a thinker, showing that you don't always know, are curious and sometimes puzzled, and can think and find out. • Encourage open-ended thinking by not settling on the first ideas: *What else is possible?* • Always respect children's efforts and ideas, so they feel safe to take a risk with a new idea. • Talking aloud helps children to think and control what they do. Model self-talk, describing your actions in play. • Give children time to talk and think. • Value questions, talk, and many possible responses, without rushing toward answers too quickly. • Support children's interests over time, reminding them of previous approaches and encouraging them to make connections between their experiences. • Model the creative process, showing your thinking about some of the many possible ways forward. • Sustained shared thinking helps children to explore ideas and make links. Follow children's lead in conversation, and think about things together. • Encourage children to describe problems they encounter, and to suggest ways to solve the problem. • Show and talk about strategies – how to do things – including problem-solving, thinking and learning. • Give feedback and help children to review their own progress and learning. Talk with children about what they are doing, how they plan to do it, what worked well and what they would change next time. • Model the plan–do–review process yourself.	• In planning activities, ask yourself: *Is this an opportunity for children to find their own ways to represent and develop their own ideas?* Avoid children just reproducing someone else's ideas. • Build in opportunities for children to play with materials before using them in planned tasks. • Play is a key opportunity for children to think creatively and flexibly, solve problems and link ideas. Establish the enabling conditions for rich play: space, time, flexible resources, choice, control, warm and supportive relationships. • Recognisable and predictable routines help children to predict and make connections in their experiences. • Routines can be flexible, while still basically orderly. • Plan linked experiences that follow the ideas children are really thinking about. • Use mind-maps to represent thinking together. • Develop a learning community which focuses on **how** and not just what we are learning.

Children develop at their own rates, and in their own ways. The development statements and their order should not be taken as necessary steps for individual children. They should not be used as checklists. The age/stage bands overlap because these are not fixed age boundaries but suggest a typical range of development.

Figure 2.4 Characteristics of effective learning in the Development Matters guidance

- keeping on trying

- enjoying achieving what they set out to do.

- **Creating and thinking critically** is broken down into:

  - having their own ideas

  - making links

  - choosing ways to do things.

The development tables

You'll find the development tables on pages 8–46 of the guidance. It's important to note that the age/stage bands overlap. This is because babies and children develop at different rates and in their own ways. The age/stage bands are not fixed age boundaries, but they do suggest a typical range of development. *The development statements and their order are not necessary steps for every child and should not be used as checklists for development.* For instance, some babies never crawl – they may shuffle around efficiently on their bottom instead – before moving on to walking.

The first page of the development tables is annotated for you on page 43 and shows how the various features of the EYFS framework are pulled together throughout the document.

How to use the Development Matters guidance in practice

In Part 3 of this book you'll explore each of the areas of learning and development in detail. You'll find out about activities which promote the early learning goals, with links to the Development Matters guidance. The links demonstrate how you can use the guidance in practice on a daily basis. You'll also learn about using the guidance to inform observation and assessment in Part 4 of this book ... so keep reading!

❗ *Don't forget*

The development tables in the Development Matters guidance tell you what you can expect to observe children learning from birth to 5 years, and what you can do to support this learning through your interactions with children and the environment you provide.

The areas of learning

The early learning goal

Personal, Social and Emotional Development: Making relationships

		A Unique Child: observing what a child is learning	Positive Relationships: what adults could do	Enabling Environments: what adults could provide
Birth – 11 months		• Enjoys the company of others and seeks contact with others from birth. • Gazes at faces and copies facial movements. e.g. sticking out tongue, opening mouth and widening eyes. • Responds when talked to, for example, moves arms and legs, changes facial expression, moves body and makes mouth movements. • Recognises and is most responsive to main carer's voice: face brightens, activity increases when familiar carer appears. • Responds to what carer is paying attention to, e.g. following their gaze. • Likes cuddles and being held: calms, snuggles in, smiles, gazes at carer's face or strokes carer's skin.	• Make sure babies have their own special person in the setting, who knows them really well and understands their wants and needs. • Tune in sensitively to babies, and provide warm, loving, consistent care, responding quickly to babies' needs. • Hold and handle babies, since sensitive touch helps to build security and attachment. • Ensure that the key person or buddy is available to greet a young baby at the beginning of the session, and to hand them over to parents at the end of a session, so the young baby is supported and communication with parents is maintained. • Engage in playful interactions that encourage young babies to respond to, or mimic, adults. • Follow the baby's lead by repeating vocalisations, mirroring movements and showing the baby that you are 'listening' fully. • Notice when babies turn away, signalling their need for less stimulation. • Discover from parents the copying games that their babies enjoy, and use these as the basis for your play. • Talk with babies about special people, such as their family members, e.g. grandparents.	• Ensure staff are aware of the importance of attachment in relationships. • Ensure the key person is paired with a 'buddy' who knows the baby and family as well, and can step in when necessary. • At times of transition (such as shift changes) make sure staff greet and say goodbye to babies and their carers. This helps to develop secure and trusting three-way relationships. • Plan to have one-to-one time to interact with young babies when they are in an alert and responsive state and willing to engage. • Display photos of family and other special people. • Share knowledge about languages with staff and parents and make a poster or book of greetings in all languages used within the setting and the community. • Repeat greetings at the start and end of each session, so that young babies recognise and become familiar with these daily rituals.
8-20 months		• Seeks to gain attention in a variety of ways, drawing others into social interaction. • Builds relationships with special people. • Is wary of unfamiliar people. • Interacts with others and explores new situations when supported by familiar person. • Shows interest in the activities of others and responds differently to children and adults, e.g. may be more interested in watching children than adults or may pay more attention when children talk to them.		
16-26 months		• Plays alongside others. • Uses a familiar adult as a secure base from which to explore independently in new environments, e.g. ventures away to play and interact with others, but returns for a cuddle or reassurance if becomes anxious. • Plays cooperatively with a familiar adult, e.g. rolling a ball back and forth.	• Involve all children in welcoming and caring for one another. • Give your full attention when young children look to you for a response. • Enable children to explore by providing a secure base for them. • Help young children to understand the feelings of others by labelling emotions such as sadness or happiness.	• Play name games to welcome children to the setting and help them get to know each other and the staff. • Regularly evaluate the way you respond to different children. • Ensure there are opportunities for the child to play alongside others and play cooperative games with a familiar adult. • Provide matching items to encourage adult and child to mimic each other in a cooperative game. e.g. two identical musical instruments.

Overlapping age bands

Statements outlining the development you are likely to observe within the age band

These columns are linked to the characteristics of effective learning and the EYFS themes/principles

Children develop at their own rates, and in their own ways. The development statements and their order should not be taken as necessary steps for individual children. They should not be used as checklists. The age/stage bands overlap because these are not fixed age boundaries but suggest a typical range of development.

Figure 2.5 Development table excerpt from the Development Matters guidance

3 Guide to the learning and development requirements

Learning and development requirements

Section 1 of the EYFS framework defines the EYFS learning and development requirements, that is 'what providers must do, working in partnership with parents and/or carers, to promote the learning and development of all children in their care, and to ensure they are ready for school'.

The learning and development requirements within the EYFS framework have been 'informed by the best available evidence on how children learn and reflect the broad range of skills, knowledge and attitudes children need as foundations for good future progress. Early years providers must guide the development of children's capabilities with a view to ensuring that children in their care complete the EYFS ready to benefit fully from the opportunities ahead of them.

The EYFS learning and development requirements comprise:

- the seven areas of learning and development and the educational programmes (as stated on page 5 of the EYFS framework)

- the early learning goals (the ELGs), which summarise the knowledge, skills and understanding that all young children should have gained by the end of the reception year

- the assessment requirements – when and how practitioners must assess children's achievements, and when and how they should discuss children's progress with parents and/or carers. (For information on assessment see Part 4 of this book.)

The areas of learning and development and the ELGs

You may like to go back to pages 22–24 in Part 1, where the areas of learning and development were first introduced, to refresh your memory before reading Part 3. In this part of the book, we will look at each of the seven areas in turn. For each area, the following information is provided:

- **The requirements of the EYFS** – that is, the activities and experiences that practitioners need to provide to promote each area of learning.

- **The early learning goals (ELGs)** – each area of learning has two or three ELGs, which set out the level of progress most children should be expected to have attained by the end of the EYFS. The ELGs are stated in full.

- **Activity suggestions** – for each age group (from birth to 60+ months), as specified within the Development Matters in the Early Years Foundation Stage guidance, suggestions for activities which promote achievement of different aspects of each ELG are provided. For each ELG, a more detailed, step-by-step 'activity in focus' is also included for one of the age ranges. The 'activities in focus' are intended to give a flavour of the kinds of activity you may provide to promote aspects of each ELG. (It would be impossible to provide activities to promote the ELGs in their entirety within the pages available as practitioners will spend several years providing numerous, varied activities for children to achieve this.) As you work through the activity suggestions provided for each area of learning, you will find it helpful to refer to the corresponding section of the Development Matters guidance.

- **Excerpts from observations** and **examples of practical tasks and resources** that you can use in your day-to-day work with children to promote the overarching principles of the EYFS (i.e. 'a unique child', 'positive relationships' and 'enabling environments').

❗ *Don't forget*

— —

The overarching principles of the EYFS are dealt with in more detail in Part 1. Refer back to pages 22–24 if you need to refresh your memory. The Development Matters guidance also links to these overarching principles.

The prime and specific areas of learning

As outlined in Part 1 of the book, within the EYFS practitioners must consider the individual needs, interests, and stage of development of each child in their care, and must use this information to plan a challenging and enjoyable experience for each child in all of the areas of learning and development.

Practitioners working with the youngest children are expected to focus strongly on the three prime areas:

- Communication and language
- Physical development
- Personal, social and emotional development.

The prime areas are the basis for successful learning in the four specific areas:

- Literacy
- Mathematics
- Understanding the world
- Expressive arts and design.

The three prime areas reflect the key skills all children need to be able to develop and learn effectively, and become ready for school. As children grow in confidence and ability within the three prime areas, the balance will shift towards a more equal focus on all the areas of learning and development.

> **❶ Don't forget**
>
> If a child's progress in any prime area throughout the early years gives you cause for concern, you must discuss this with the child's parents and/or carers, and agree how to support the child. You must consider whether a child may have a special educational need or disability which requires specialist support. You should work with families to help them access relevant services from other agencies, as appropriate.

How should the areas of learning and development be implemented?

The EYFS framework states that 'each area of learning and development must be implemented through planned, purposeful play and a mix of adult-led and child-initiated activity'. Play is essential for children's development. It builds their confidence through:

- exploration
- thinking about problems
- relating to others.

❗ Don't forget

Children learn by leading their own play and by taking part in play which is guided by adults.

Ask Miranda!

Q: Is there guidance on how many activities should be led by children and how many led by adults? I work with children aged 3 to 5 years and I don't know how many activities of each type I should be planning.

A: The EYFS framework acknowledges that practitioners need to make ongoing judgements about the balance between activities led by children, and activities led or guided by adults ... As children grow older and as their development allows, it is expected that the balance will gradually shift towards more activities led by adults, to help children prepare for more formal learning, ready for Year 1. It's important to remember, though, that children have until the end of Reception year to be prepared for formal learning. The EYFS framework also states that practitioners must respond to each child's emerging needs and interests, and this most certainly requires plenty of child-led opportunities.

Ask Miranda!

Q: How should the areas of learning and development be implemented with children whose home language is not English?

A: The EYFS framework states that, for children whose home language is not English, providers must:

- take reasonable steps to provide opportunities for children to develop and use their home language in play and learning, supporting their language development at home

- ensure that children have sufficient opportunities to learn and reach a good standard in English language during the EYFS

- assess children's communication, language and literacy skills in English and, if a child does not have a strong grasp of the English language, explore the child's skills in the home language with parents and/or carers to establish whether there is cause for concern about language delay.

Characteristics of effective learning

According to the EYFS framework, practitioners must reflect the *three* characteristics of effective learning in their practice. This is important because the characteristics reflect the different ways that children learn. You therefore need to consider and provide a range of effective ways for each individual child within your care to learn. The three characteristics of effective learning are:

• **playing and exploring** – children investigate and experience things, and 'have a go'

• **active learning** – children concentrate and keep on trying if they encounter difficulties, and enjoy achievements

• **creating and thinking critically** – children have and develop their own ideas, make links between ideas, and develop strategies for doing things.

The three characteristics of effective learning should be promoted throughout all the seven areas of learning and development. The table on page 49 shows some examples of how this can be put into practice.

❗ Don't forget

In planning and guiding children's activities, practitioners must reflect on the different ways that children learn and consider these in their practice.

Area of learning and development	Characteristic of effective learning	Example
Understanding the world	Playing and exploring	Daisy and Josh take magnifying glasses outside and search for insects in the garden. They are playing and exploring.
Physical development	Active learning	Tyrone is trying to use the pedals on a bike. His feet keep slipping off so he's stopping and starting a lot. He keeps putting them back on and going a bit further. He keeps on trying when he encounters difficulties.
Expressive arts and design	Creating and thinking critically	Kyra wants to make a flag to wave outside in the wind. She asks a practitioner if she can get a stick, some paper and some sticky tape. She is having and developing her own ideas, making links between ideas, and developing strategies for doing things.

Prime areas

Communication and language

According to the EYFS framework, communication and language development involves giving children opportunities to:

- experience a rich language environment

- develop their confidence and skills in expressing themselves

- speak and listen in a range of situations.

Ask Miranda!

Q: What does 'giving children opportunities to experience a rich language environment' mean?

A: A child's 'language environment' simply means the language a child is exposed to on an everyday basis. A rich language environment is essentially one in which adults talk with children frequently, using a wide, age-appropriate vocabulary. Children are encouraged to express themselves, so adults are also doing a lot of listening. (Examples of this are included on the following pages.) Adults make good use of open-ended questions, but it's important not to overdo these or a child may feel overwhelmed. (As a general rule, use more statements than questions in your conversations with children.)

Why is communication and language a prime area of learning?

Communication and language skills underpin much of children's development. This is because the ability to communicate – that is, the ability to both understand what is said and to be understood – enables children to do so much. If a child cannot understand and/or be understood, overall development is affected. The following diagram shows the areas of development that are supported by children's speech, language and communication skills:

Figure 3.1 Areas of development supported by children's communication and language skills

We'll look at each area in turn:

Learning

Learning occurs when children receive, process and then use information. Information is received both non-verbally and verbally.

Non-verbal information

For instance, if a child touches a radiator that is on, they will receive information that it is hot when their hand feels uncomfortable. They may then process the information and make the connection that touching the radiator leads to discomfort. If they then use the information, they will avoid touching the radiator again.

Verbal information

Much of children's learning (receiving, processing and using information), however, is received from verbal communication. Children learn from what is said directly to them and what they hear. Consider this example:

- Alicia doesn't have a garden or houseplants at home, so her first experience of watering plants happens at pre-school. The practitioner explains to her that the plants will die without water. Two days later, Alicia visits her Gran, who has a houseplant on the kitchen window sill. Alicia says to her, 'Can I water your plant? Or it might die'. This shows that Alicia had processed the information given to her by the pre-school practitioner, and used it in another context.

Children can use their communication skills to ask questions, a key way of learning throughout life. There's evidence that language also assists the processing of information – speaking aloud helps young children to think. You can learn more about 'language for thinking' and about the role of questioning in creative learning in the 'Activity in focus – It's a small world' on page 64.

Emotional development

A key aspect of children's emotional development is the increasing ability to recognise, understand and express their own emotions. Through language development, children learn a label for the emotions they feel – 'upset', 'angry' and so on. They can then go on to talk about their feelings. Babies cannot control their emotions, and toddlers characteristically find this difficult, hence temper tantrums at this age.

But young children generally tend to gain more control of their emotions as their language develops. The ability to communicate feelings through words seemingly relieves frustration at not understanding their emotions and not having them understood by others.

Behavioural development

Behavioural development is strongly linked to language and communication. The word 'no' is generally learned while children are still babies. This is important because understanding the meaning of 'no' helps to keep children safe, as well as teaching them how to behave in socially acceptable ways. Language acquisition also enables young children to communicate their own likes, dislikes and preferences. This leads to a decline in the impulsive behaviour linked to frustration.

The next developmental step is for children to understand the information they're given about the *reasons* for behaving in certain ways, to process the information and to use it. For instance, if a child is told not to touch a neighbour's dog, they are likely to learn just that. However, if a child receives an explanation as to *why* they shouldn't touch *any* dogs they come across without permission from the owner and their parent or carer, they have the opportunity to understand and to process. In the future they may then use the information by refraining from touching a strange dog in the street. The process of talking about rules, behaviour and consequences also helps children to think about and understand them.

Social development

You've learned how part of children's emotional development is to understand and express their own emotions. This is closely linked to social development, in which children learn to recognise and understand the emotions and responses of other people, including whether or not they approve of the child's own behaviour. This enables children to learn about what it is socially acceptable to say and to do. The information children receive will be partly verbal, but they will also be learning to read people's body language and facial expressions. Toddlers happily play in each other's company without conversing but, as they reach around three years of age, children typically begin interacting with one another on a new social level. Talking becomes increasingly important to peer relationships and play.

> **❗ Don't forget**
> -
> **Speech, language and communication difficulties**
>
> Practitioners should learn to recognise when children have speech, language and communication difficulties. This is important because the earlier a difficulty can be detected, the earlier a child can get the specialist support that they need. Some children with minor or temporary difficulties progress quickly when they receive the appropriate help. Children may experience difficulties speaking, hearing or understanding, or they may lack a general interest in communicating.

> **❗ Don't forget**
> -
> Practitioners must be sensitive to the communication needs of children. It may be necessary to adapt communication methods to suit children's needs. It is helpful to find out what you can about specific difficulties, and for the setting to liaise with families and other professionals about communication strategies.

The ELGs

There are three ELGs for this prime area of learning and development:

1. Listening and attention (see page 54)

2. Understanding (see page 60)

3. Speaking (see page 66)

Each one is explained in detail in the relevant section that follows.

Listening and attention

◉ Early learning goal

Listening and attention Children listen attentively in a range of situations. They listen to stories, accurately anticipating key events and responding to what they hear with relevant comments, questions or actions. They give their attention to what others say and respond appropriately, while engaged in another activity.

Activity ideas

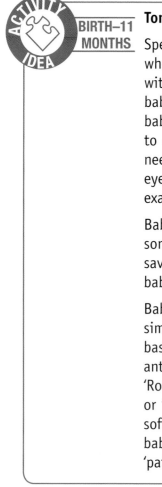

BIRTH–11 MONTHS

Tones

Spend plenty of time talking to babies in a lively tone when they are content, and soothe them reassuringly with gentle tones when they are distressed. Ensure babies can see your face – make eye-contact with babies when communicating with them. An ideal time to communicate is when attending to babies' care needs. The baby and carer can look into each other's eyes during nappy changing and bottle feeding, for example.

Babies respond well to playfulness, and higher, sing-song tones help to convey this. But it's important to save these for the appropriate times – avoid exciting babies at sleep and feeding times.

Babies enjoy responding to repeated sounds, so sing simple songs and share rhymes on a one-to-one basis. Babies enjoy getting to know them and like to anticipate the fun endings to old favourites such as 'Round and round the garden' (that ends in a tickle), or 'Horsey, horsey' (that ends with the child being softly bounced up and down on the carer's knee). As babies learn to clap, encourage them to join in with 'pat-a-cake' rhymes.

Figure 3.2 Make eye-contact with babies when communicating with them

---

❗ *Don't forget*

- -

You can read and tell stories to the youngest of children – it is never too early! Babies enjoy listening to the rise and fall of your voice long before they understand the words you are saying.

ACTIVITY IDEA

8–20 MONTHS

Move to the beat

Background music can actually be detrimental to young children's learning and development. It's thought to distract their focus away from other stimuli in the environment. It may also tire or overwhelm them. So only use music or other recordings in limited bursts and for particular purposes. This also helps children to show interest and to listen when recordings are played.

One particular purpose of using music is to introduce young children to the sound of a beat. This can be truly delightful for both children and the practitioner, as children in this age range will begin to show signs of appreciating music (or even just a rhythm) in a new way – they will often enjoy moving their whole bodies to the beat of a sound they enjoy.

You can encourage this by showing that you are enjoying their reaction. You might smile for instance, or mirror their movement back to them by nodding your head along to the beat. You can also clap along, which helps to emphasise where the beat falls.

Development matters!

A unique child: observing what children are learning

Excerpt from a checklist observation of a 9-month-old baby which shows the progress they are making in the area of communication and language:

Activity	Yes	No	Date	Observer's comments
Knows own name	✔		24/9/12	
Initiates range of sounds	✔		24/9/12	Longer strings of babbling sounds made
Enjoys listening to rhymes and songs	✔		24/9/12	Greatly enjoys this
Listens to carer talk then responds with own sounds	✔		24/9/12	Leaves conversational gaps and waits for carer to respond

What noise does it make?

16–24 MONTHS

Share picture books on a one-to-one basis. Young children enjoy learning the names of objects they see in the pictures, so point to them and use word labels such as 'ball' or 'car'. Children also enjoy learning the sounds that familiar animals and objects make, so build opportunities for this into your one-to-one time together. For instance, you may point at a picture and say, 'Dog. And the dog goes, woof, woof!' As children begin to pick this up you can ask them simple questions such as, 'What does that duck say?' Be prepared to answer yourself though if the child doesn't respond, for example 'It says quack, quack!'

You can also take the opportunity to introduce sounds to general play. For example, when playing alongside a child with a car you may say, 'vroom!' or 'beep beep!' This is an important way to introduce and encourage the use of sound in imaginary play.

Visual aids

22–36 MONTHS

Visual aids, such as puppets, dolls and soft toys, are an excellent way to encourage children in this age range to pay attention to stories, rhymes and songs. They also promote reaction and interaction.

You can make wide use of other props too. For example, you might use the appropriate real fruits and vegetables as visual aids when telling the well-known *Hungry Caterpillar* story. Where possible, make the aids available for children to play with freely after the story or singing sessions, so they can re-enact and explore stories and songs in their own ways.

Development matters!

Positive relationships: what adults could do

Jason is a new practitioner working in a nursery with children aged 30 to 50 months. At a recent team meeting, it was agreed that Jason and his colleagues should put together some story sacks. Jason has been given the task of creating the first one. He's also been asked to let the parents and carers know about story sacks, and what the setting will be doing with them, by writing a brief introduction for inclusion in the setting's next newsletter.

Jason hasn't made a story sack before, so he starts by doing a bit of research. He finds a useful description of what a story sack is on the Literacy Trust website. It says, 'A story sack is a large cloth bag containing a favourite children's book with supporting materials to stimulate language activities and make reading a memorable and enjoyable experience.' Jason decides to quote this in the piece he'll write for the newsletter.

On the same website, he also finds fantastic instructions for making and using a story sack for the story *We're Going on a Bear Hunt*. The setting has this, and it's a firm favourite with the children. Jason decides to follow the instructions. Once he has his first story sack under his belt, he plans to create his own from scratch for another of the children's favourite books – *Peace At Last* by Jill Murphy.

❗ Don't forget

You can find the National Literacy Trust's information about story sacks at www.literacytrust.org.uk – just type 'story sacks' into the search box.

ACTIVITY IDEA

30–50 MONTHS

Sound circle

Choose a quiet location and ask a small group of children to sit together in a circle. Explain that you're going to listen very carefully to a sound made by one of the group, and then take it in turns to pass the sound around the circle. Start this off by making a sound yourself – choose something simple that is easy to repeat, such as 'chug, chug, chug'. Ask the child to your right if they can copy the sound. Next ask the child on their right to do the same. Repeat with the third child along. Children will now be getting the idea, and may start to take their turns spontaneously without you prompting them. Once the sound has done a full circuit, you may like to repeat it again, this time going a little bit faster.

Next, ask one of the children to make a new sound for the group to pass around. (They may need some prompts or suggestions.) Give all the children the opportunity to take on the role of the sound leader in turn.

Extension idea: As children become more familiar with this activity, you can increase the number of children playing at any one time, and make the sounds more complex by including patterns. For example, 'chug' may change to 'chug, ching' then to 'chug, ching, chang'. You can also replace verbal sounds with tapping or clapping.

Sound lotto

40–60+ MONTHS

This activity has two stages – making a sound lotto game and playing it with a group of children.

You will need:
- An audio recorder
- A camera
- A printer
- Cardboard
- Scissors and paste

What to do:

1. Talk to a small group of children about the everyday sounds that they hear within the setting, such as the sound of the doorbell, the ringing of the phone, the sound of the taps running in the bathroom, or a baby crying in the baby room.

2. Take the children on a sound hunt around the setting. Use the audio recorder to record some of the recognisable sounds, and use the camera to take photos of the object/person that makes the sound. Aim for around eight sounds.

3. Upload the photos to a computer, and make them into a montage, so they form a grid. This will create the lotto playing board. Print off one for each child. It's a good idea to mount them on card for durability. (You may choose to have them laminated later, in which case you will need to carefully round off sharp corners.)

4. Cut out some cardboard squares that are the same size as the photos. (Children will use them to cover each picture on their board as they recognise the sound made by the object/person depicted.) The task is repetitive and takes a bit of time, so it's suggested that you prepare the squares ahead of time and show them to the children, rather than involving them in the process.

5. Now you're ready to play the game. To do this, select a quiet location and give each child a lotto board. Encourage them to listen carefully as you play one of the sounds. Can they recognise it? Looking at the pictures on the boards will serve as a prompt. You can also give clues if necessary, for example 'I think we may have heard this sound in the garden ...' As children successfully identify a sound, they cover the picture with a cardboard square. The game is over when all the pictures are covered.

Development matters!

Positive relationships: what adults could do

- Childminder Richie is reading a story to two children, 3-year-old Logan and 4-year-old Amalie. Every so often he pauses to ask the children what they think will happen next. Amalie responds well to this, and makes suggestions. Logan is less forthcoming, but he's listening carefully to what Amalie has to say. Richie thinks about this, and decides that next time he will try turning a page and asking Logan to see if he can describe what's happening in the picture before he reads them the text.

Understanding

Early learning goal

Understanding: Children follow instructions involving several ideas or actions. They answer 'how' and 'why' questions about their experiences and in response to stories or events.

Activity ideas

BIRTH–11 MONTHS AND 8–20 MONTHS

Words and meanings

Help children to link words and meanings by:

- telling them the names of things and people that they point to
- pointing out real objects and pictures in books and naming them (such as cup, spoon, ball, cat, bed)
- linking words with actions to help make their meaning clear, for example, waving bye-bye, doing simple actions during simple songs and rhymes (such as 'Heads, shoulders, knees and toes')
- repeating words in context (for example, by saying 'drink' when they are lifted into a high chair)
- using the child's name to get their attention.

16–26 MONTHS

Taking action

Provide young children with plenty of opportunities to interact with stimulating resources, such as:

- toys that have features they can press, turn, lift, twist, push or pull, for instance a board book which makes the sound of the various animals depicted when a button is pressed, or traditional pop-up toys
- interesting materials, such as shiny sheets of paper or silky fabrics
- natural and artificial materials
- objects that travel, such as balls and toy cars
- objects that make sounds, such as toys with a chime or bell inside.

Also, see the information on 'heuristic play' on page 174.

❶ Don't forget

The primary way to support and extend children's communication and language is via the conversations and the interactions that you have with them. You should be talking with individual children frequently.

▶

It's important that you pitch the level of language and the words you use in line with a child's age and stage of development. Practitioners need to simplify the words they use and their sentence structure when working with babies and younger children. But by the time most children are 3, they are ready to hear more complex dialogue. They need this stimulus to increase their own vocabularies and achieve further language development. With experience, switching between levels like this becomes second nature.

Development matters!

A unique child: observing what children are learning

'Scaffolding' is the term used to describe an important technique used by practitioners to verbally give a child the support and help they need to be able to understand or complete a task that they can't manage alone. This should help them to move towards understanding or carrying out the task independently in the future. Scaffolding the child's learning is a natural part of a practitioner's role – just think about how often you prompt a child verbally. Below is an excerpt from a free description child observation which records how scaffolding effectively promotes a young child's understanding:

Practitioner approaches child.

Practitioner: It's raining today, so before we go outside we need to put on our ...?

Child: Shoes.

Practitioner: We do need our shoes on, yes. We always wear them outside, don't we? And there's something else we wear when it's raining ... We put it on and we zip it up ...?

Child: Coat!

Practitioner: That's right, we need our coats to keep us dry. And we can put our hoods up, can't we, to keep our heads dry.

Child: I need to put my coat on because it's raining outside.

Instructions

22–36 MONTHS

Within this age range, children increasingly learn to understand instructions and more complex sentences, so it's a good time to introduce more activities that rely on talk to initiate action. For example, you can involve children in tasks such as making play dough, in which instructions might include, 'Tip it all into the bowl' or 'Give it another stir'.

There are many everyday opportunities that can be used to encourage this. For instance, when tidying away you can get children to help you by asking them to sort objects into sets – for example, three different types of resource (bricks, vehicles and picture books) into three different boxes.

Development matters!

Enabling environments: what adults could provide

Specific activities aimed at promoting communication are extremely helpful, but don't forget just how important day-to-day activities are too. They provide much opportunity for conversation and interaction as well as time on a one-to-one basis.

Daily activities also present opportunities to repeat phrases and words, which is an effective way of scaffolding learning. For example, at circle time you might complete a 'today' chart everyday, which involves talking about the weather and selecting an appropriate image (the sun, a cloud etc.) to display. There are few routine activities that cannot be turned into an opportunity to encourage communication development. One of the most basic and natural ways to do this is by simply talking about an aspect of what you are doing or what is happening. For instance, when taking a child to hang up her coat on arrival, you could engage in a guessing game about how she got to the setting that day – did she walk, ride in a car, catch the bus etc?

It's a small world

Small world toys are common in most settings, but within high quality environments they will be presented in exciting ways to maximise potential creativity in children within this age range. They can be used to promote the use of language for thinking, opening up a whole world of conversation about what children are doing and why. The following activity promotes creativity through playing with toy vehicles.

You will need:
- A train set
- Construction materials, including corrugated cars and sticky tape
- A large sheet of strong paper
- Mark-making materials, such as crayons, pencils
- Interlocking bricks

What to do:
1. Set up the train set.
2. If you model making your own tunnel for a train to pass through from construction materials, such as corrugated card and tape, children are likely to follow suit. (The aim here is to inspire children rather than to instruct them to copy you.)
3. Make use of open-ended questions to promote the use of language for thinking – 'How will you make the card into a tunnel shape?'
4. Set out mark-making resources and a large sheet of paper with the toy cars so children can draw their own roads – much more creative than tipping the cars out onto a readymade play mat. If you usually set up toy cars on the floor, experiment with placing them on a table instead, and vice versa if you usually provide them on the table. This can really change the way in which children interact with the resources.
5. Introduce the interlocking bricks so children can make garages or buildings to stand along the roadside. Again, you can model these ideas and use open-ended questions to promote language for thinking.

Extension ideas: Set up the small world farmyard in a tray of real soil and turf; or try using sand, water and shells to recreate a sea-bed in which children can play with small world marine life creatures.

Imaginary areas

Creative use of imaginary areas can effectively encourage role play in which children, acting characters that they have created, use rich language to talk about and act out scenarios. This promotes use of language for thinking as well as communication.

Make sure your role-play areas feature real objects and artefacts to enrich imaginary play, such as saucepans in the home corner for real pasta 'cooking' and a real (disconnected!) telephone to play with.

Change the focus of imaginary areas regularly and provide ever-expanding opportunities to bring the real world into the setting. For instance, if the area is a corner shop, provide real cans and packets of food that can be sold, along with real fruit and vegetables. Borrow a price-labelling gun and provide real money for use in the shop. If the area is a post office, make real junk mail and stamps available.

Figure 3.3 Make sure role-play areas feature real objects, such as a telephone

Speaking

❗ Don't forget

For young children, rich everyday language 'activities' are much more valuable than one-off, novelty experiences.

Activity ideas

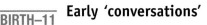

BIRTH–11 MONTHS

Early 'conversations'

Join in with babies' playful babbles, repeating sounds back to them. Continue to talk to babies frequently and engage them in 'conversation' by talking to them, then pausing to allow the baby to 'reply', then 'answer' them once again. Respond with delight by your facial expressions, body language and your speech when babies communicate their delight to you. Show sympathy in your facial expressions, body language and your speech when babies communicate their distress to you. Remember to talk *with* babies, not *to* them.

Extension idea: Look out for signs that babies are using sounds for deliberate communication around the 6- to 11-month stage – take care to respond to this to encourage babies to repeat their efforts. Sadly, evidence shows that if children's efforts to communicate are not responded to, they will try to communicate less frequently. If this continues, they will eventually stop trying altogether and may become much less responsive when others communicate with them.

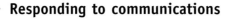

Responding to communications

Respond encouragingly to babies' vocalisations (which will increasingly sound like speech) and children's first words (which are usually spoken around 12 months), so that they are motivated to keep talking to you.

Show interest in what children have to say. Ensure that you reply to them whenever they talk to you. Take what they say seriously, even if words are missing, or you are not sure what is meant. Do try your best to interpret the words that children say though – it's important for you to be familiar with the language a child uses to refer to favourite objects – for instance, a child may say 'brum' for car, or 'Da' for Daddy. Find out from their parents any particular words that they use for specific items that are of importance to them – for example, they may say 'blankie' when they are tired and want their security blanket from home.

Take note of children's gestures too – they often use them to fill in the gaps in their vocabularies. Pointing at objects of interest or things they want is a good example of this. It's important that children feel their efforts at communicating meaning are worthwhile.

Share first picture books on a one-to-one basis. Young children enjoy learning the names of objects they see in the pictures. As they become aware of body language, children also enjoy simple songs with actions they can copy – they can use these to fill the gaps when they have not yet learned all of the words. Sing them slowly so children have sufficient time to join in.

Extension idea: Give babies and young children plenty of opportunities to interact with their peers and slightly older children if possible, for example in shared singing, music or story times and shared free play, where appropriate.

ACTIVITY IDEA

16–26 MONTHS

Running commentary

Talk to young children in a running commentary style about what you're doing, what they're doing or what's going on around you – this can be a wonderful way to both engage and include them, and to expose them to new, rich language. It's also an effective way to introduce them to different types of everyday words (nouns, verbs and adjectives). Point out what other children are doing to help a child to learn and use the names of their peers.

Capturing interest

This complements the running commentary method, because you can point out what's going on around you to babies and young children, using an excited, engaging tone and begin to ask some simple questions. A favourite activity is to look out of the window together and see what's going on in the world. For example, you might say, 'Look Ruby, the postman's coming! Do you think he's got a letter for us?' You can also draw their attention to an object and motivate them to explore it. A good way of doing this is to do something interesting with it. So instead of just lifting a child up to look at a homemade mobile fashioned from old CDs, you can give it a nudge so that it moves and catches the light and say, 'Look, it's spinning …'

22–36 MONTHS

Bodies

At this age, children are beginning to become more independent in their own personal care, so it's a good time to plan activities which help children to learn new words associated with their bodies in the context of play and activities. Why not try the following:

- Sing songs with actions such as 'Heads, shoulders, knees and toes' and 'Here we go round the mulberry bush' (with verses including, 'This is the way we brush our teeth/put on our clothes/comb our hair/wash our hands' etc.)
- Help children to associate words, feelings and facial expressions. For instance, after running around outside with the children you may put your hand to your face and say, 'I'm feeling hot! Are you feeling hot?' (See also information on the use of persona resources in the 'Understanding the world' section on pages 164–165.)
- Involve a child in helping you dress up a favourite toy – 'Can you put a hat on her head?'

❗ Don't forget

Encourage parents of children who have English as an additional language to share favourite rhymes and songs in the child's home language with you. You can use these in your work with both the individual child and the group as a whole.

Development matters!

A unique child: observing what children are learning

Excerpt from a checklist observation of a 24-month-old child showing progress in communication and language skills.

Activity	Yes	No	Date	Observer's comments
Will often name objects on sight	✔		2/10/12	
Joins two words together	✔		2/10/12	Occasionally, e.g. 'shoes on'
Uses people's names	✔		2/10/12	Uses names of key carers and siblings

ACTIVITY IN FOCUS

30-50 MONTHS

Photo diary

You will need:

- A camera
- Access to a computer and printer
- Wall display space
- An audio recorder

What to do:

1. Talk to children about the fact that their parents and carers are very interested in everything they do at your setting. Tell them you think it will be fun to record the activities they do during the morning in a special display of photographs, which they can help you take throughout the session. Parents and carers can view these later.

2. During the session, take photos of key activities, such as various free-play opportunities, circle time, story time.

3. Next, upload the photos to a computer and print them out. Share them with the children, and enlist them in helping you to stick the photos onto the display board.

4. Ask each of the children to tell you something relevant to the display, such as something about an activity (for example, 'We had a story about a funny dog') or perhaps something that they've noticed in the photo ('Ben's got blue painty hands!'). Record this on an audio recorder. (If a child is reluctant to be recorded, they can tell you something to say on their behalf.)

5. Make the audio recorder available alongside the display.

6. When visitors to the room and parents/carers arrive, encourage children to show them the display and play them the recording.

You may like to ask the parents of children who are learning English as an additional language to record some commentary for you in their home language.

Development matters!

Enabling environments: what adults could provide

Resources to support speaking include:

- toy telephones, walkie-talkies, communication boards
- a broad range of interesting activities and experiences
- interesting sensory stimulation – things to see, feel, touch, smell, taste, hear
- comfortable areas for children to relax and talk in
- books and visual aids
- recordings of music and other sounds, story CDs
- sequencing cards/pictures
- puppets, dolls, soft toys, masks.

40–60+ MONTHS

Interest tables and feely bags

A key part of supporting and extending young children's skills is providing them with engaging information and activities that motivate them to communicate and give them something to talk about. For example, interest tables are an excellent way to get children talking about new information and the objects available for exploration, as the following Development matters! feature shows.

'Feely bags' are a good example of an activity which promotes communication and use of descriptive language. Simply place a familiar object – such as an

▶

apple – in a drawstring bag. Without looking, a child puts their hand inside and describes what they can feel. The group try to guess what the object is – you can give a series of clues if necessary. Once the object is revealed, place a new one in the bag (without children seeing what it is) and invite another child to have a turn.

❗ Don't forget

As part of your preparation for this activity, you could learn the names of the objects to be concealed in a feely bag in the various home languages of children attending the setting. These can then be introduced during the activity.

⬢ Development matters!

Positive relationships: what adults could do

Iona works at a children's centre. It's her turn to organise the interest table this week, and she wants to use it to help expand children's vocabularies. She also wants to tie in the table with the setting's current theme – autumn.

She decides to take a small group of children for a walk with her and a colleague. They collect a range of fallen leaves and some conkers. When they get back, Iona arranges these on the table. She adds some magnifying glasses so that children can look closely at the items. She soon has some eager children exploring them. They ask Iona where the leaves and conkers came from, and why they fell off the trees. Iona gives them the information. She then asks the children some questions – what do the leaves and conkers feel like? What do they smell like? What similarities and differences are there in colour, shape etc? Why do they think some of the leaves are brown and brittle?

When evaluating the activity, Iona notes that not only did the table promote rich use of vocabulary but the discussions also encouraged children to use language for thinking.

Physical development

According to the EYFS framework, physical development involves providing opportunities for young children to:

- be active and interactive

- develop their coordination, control, and movement.

Children must also be helped to understand the importance of physical activity, and to make healthy choices in relation to food.

Ask Miranda!

Q: What is 'physical development'?

A: Physical development is the development of controlled physical movement. As part of their physical development, children acquire skills to help control their movement.

Physical reflexes

The neonate (newly born baby) has reflexes. These are physical movements or reactions that they make without consciously intending to do so. For example, the neonate will move their head in search of the mother's nipple or the teat of a bottle when their lips or cheek are touched (known as rooting), and they will also suck and swallow milk. These reflexes help the baby to feed, and therefore survive. You may have experienced the grasp reflex – a baby will clasp their fingers around yours if you touch their palm. You will probably have seen the startle reflex too – a startled baby will make a fist and their arms will move away from their body. This often occurs if there is a loud noise, or if the baby wakes suddenly. The standing and walking reflex can be seen if a baby is held upright in the standing position with their feet resting on a firm surface, such as the floor. They will make stepping movements with their legs.

Gross motor skills

'Gross motor skills' are an aspect of physical development. The term is used to refer to whole-body movements such as:

- sitting up

- crawling

- walking
- kicking a ball.

These skills develop rapidly during a child's first five years.

Locomotive movements

Sometimes, practitioners separate out an additional category of physical development – 'locomotive movements'. The term is used to describe activities relating to balance and travelling, such as walking, running and standing on one leg. Other practitioners include these in the gross motor skills category, as described above.

Crawling   Sitting from lying down   Bear-walking

Walking with two hands held   Walking with one hand held   Walking alone

Figure 3.4 Gross motor skills involved in the development of walking

Fine motor skills

'Fine motor skills' are another aspect of physical development. The term is used to refer to delicate, manipulative movements that are made with the fingers. Fine motor skills and the development of vision are linked. This is often referred to as 'hand–eye coordination'. Fine motor skills and hand–eye coordination are used when a child is threading cotton reels, for example – the child will look carefully at the position of the hole in the reel, and manipulate the string accordingly.

> **❗ Don't forget**
>
> Physical movement and action have an important part to play in children's learning because children's bodies are developing alongside their brains. In other words, children learn through movement and action. Unless they need sleep or rest, the amount of time that young children spend being sedentary (inactive) should be minimised.

Why is physical development a prime area of learning?

Physical development skills underpin much of children's development. According to the EYFS framework, this area reflects the key skills and capabilities all children need to develop and learn effectively, and become ready for school.

According to the Tickell Review, physical development supports personal, social and emotional development as increasing physical control provides experiences of the self as an active agent in the environment, promoting growth in confidence and awareness of control. It supports communication and language because a child who can effectively use large movements, gestures and the fine movement involved in speech is able to convey messages to others.

Active learning in this area should be hands-on, whole-bodied and movement-based.

> **❗ Don't forget**
>
> Practitioners should aim to create a movement-rich environment – opportunities to move in many varied ways should be embedded within the setting's everyday routines, activities and experiences.

The ELGs

There are two ELGs for this prime area of learning and development:

1. Moving and handling (see page 76)

2. Health and self-care (see page 90).

Each one is explained in detail in the relevant section that follows.

Moving and handling

> 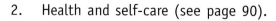 **Early learning goal**
>
> **Moving and handling**: Children show good control and coordination in large and small movements. They move confidently in a range of ways, safely negotiating space. They handle equipment and tools effectively, including pencils for writing.

Activity ideas

BIRTH–11 MONTHS

Body awareness

It's important for practitioners to help young children to become aware of their own bodies. A fun way of doing this is to introduce touch and movement through songs and rhymes. You can bounce a baby on your knee while you share some music, for instance, or hold their hands and gently move them to the rhythm. Or you might touch the palm of a baby's hand while reciting 'Round and round the garden'. (See the activity 'Tones' in the 'Communication and language' section on page 54 for other suggestions of songs and rhymes to use with babies.)

You can also help babies to understand the difference between their own body and the bodies of others by engaging in play that involves passing objects between you and the baby. You will find that babies go through a stage of development where they will naturally offer you objects, such as a rattle they've been playing with. You can show some interest in the object and then pass it back to them, creating a two-way exchange. This is highlighted in the following Development matters! feature.

Development matters!

Development matters!

8–20 MONTHS

Gloop

Babies and young children in this age range enjoy the sensation of touching a range of materials, which they will manipulate and feel in a number of different ways. You can promote this by providing 'gloop' (a mixture of cornflour and water) for them to explore. For this age range, gloop is best presented in shallow trays.

Gloop is a unique material and therefore quite hard to describe! It looks like a liquid, but when touched it feels solid. It's possible to dig your fingers into gloop, or to pick up a fistful of it. Yet within moments of doing so, it will turn to liquid and run from your fingers or hands, only to reset once more when it drips back onto the tray. Even the youngest children in this age range will be able to enjoy this experience by simply patting at a tray of gloop with their hands or poking it with their fingers. Older children in the age range may also enjoy the opportunity to put their bare feet in a tray of gloop, and feel it running away between their toes – this is perhaps best done outside as it is likely to be messy!

You will need:
- A 500g box of cornflour
- A jug of water (approx) 350ml
- Food colouring (optional)
- A mixing bowl
- A tablespoon
- Shallow trays
- Aprons
- Plastic table cloths
- A damp cloth

What to do:

1. To make gloop, mix a 500g box of cornflour with approximately 350ml of water in a mixing bowl. Exactly how much water is needed depends of the type of cornflour, so add it slowly, a bit at a time. You're aiming for a consistency where the gloop feels solid when first touched, but soon dissolves to a liquid which drips from the mixing spoon. (If you add too much water, the mixture will become a liquid. If you don't add enough water, it will stay solid.) If you wish, add a few drops of food colouring into the water and stir it in before adding to the cornflour.

2. Place the gloop in shallow trays.

3. Before giving the trays to children, make sure that you protect their clothing and the surfaces around them with aprons, plastic tablecloths etc.

4. During play, remember that babies and young children will take everything to their mouths for exploration, so supervise them carefully to ensure that they do not eat the gloop.

5. Some children may be a bit wary of touching the gloop. You can play yourself to give them some confidence, and you may like to provide objects they can put into the gloop if they prefer, such as a small spoon.

6. When cleaning up, a damp cloth can be used effectively to remove gloop from hard surfaces, such as table tops. This method tends to make more of a mess, however, if applied to fabrics! If gloop does get onto clothing or carpets, leave it to dry. The water will evaporate and a white powdery residue will be left behind. This can simply be brushed off.

Development matters!

Enabling environments: what adults could provide

Resources and activities within early years settings that help to promote development of gross motor skills between 12 months and 2 years include:

- throwing and rolling large balls – simple catch games, skittles
- kicking with large balls – simple kicking and receiving games
- walking, and climbing with supervision – up and down steps, on low climbing cubes
- push and pull toys – such as carts and prams, together with toys to take in and out and to transport
- ride-on toys without pedals (large wheeled toys)
- swinging and sliding on small items of playground equipment
- using low stilts
- splashing around in water – in a bath, paddling pool or swimming pool. Must be *closely supervised* at all times.

Enabling environments: what adults could provide

Children also need access to a wide range of resources and activities to support their fine motor skills and hand–eye coordination. There are many you can offer. A few staples frequently offered in early years settings for 12 to 15 months include:

- interesting objects, such as rattles, that children want to pick up, hold and explore

- different textures to grasp – hard plastic objects and soft toys or soft balls

- putting objects in and out of a simple posting box

- stacking cups and blocks of different textures: plastic, wood; soft, hard.

ACTIVITY IDEA

16–26 MONTHS

Transporting with wheels

In this age range, children enjoy pushing, pulling and riding on equipment with wheels – including trolleys, carts, buggies and vehicles such as trikes, cars and tractors (the type without pedals which children propel forwards by pushing along on the ground with their feet; many of these have storage space under a seat which lifts up). Children also enjoy transporting items from one place to another and this promotes the physical dexterity needed to pick things up, and to lift and carry. You can combine these two activities by providing resources for children to transport via their wheeled resources. For example, you could place buckets, containing items such as pebbles or toy blocks, at one end of the garden and children could transport the buckets/items to the sandpit or 'construction' area.

Extension idea: Children in this age range are beginning to make connections between their movements and the marks they make. You can draw their attention to the tyre marks they make on the ground when they play with wheeled toys, for example, after they ride through a puddle or a patch of muddy ground.

Figure 3.5 Building towers with blocks helps promote development of fine motor skills and hand–eye coordination

ACTIVITY IDEA

22–36 MONTHS

Traffic lights

Activities which involve starting and stopping and moving at variable speeds are good for children in this age range, so the game 'Traffic lights' is ideal.

Children start by running around an open space, in any direction they like. When the person leading the game calls out 'Red' everyone must stop. When they call 'Amber' everyone must walk. When they call 'Green' everyone can run again. Some children may also enjoy taking a turn at leading the game themselves.

Extension idea: You may like to extend the game by asking children to move in different ways rather than simply running or walking. For instance, you could have a round where children roll over, or crawl like a lion, or slither like a snake.

Development matters!

Enabling environments: what adults could provide

Resources that help to promote development of fine motor skills and hand–eye coordination for 2- to 3-year-olds include:

- large beads for threading
- paper and crayons for mark making, such as drawing circles
- large interlocking bricks for building
- shape sorters for identifying and sorting solid shapes
- puzzle play trays for manipulating shapes that fit together
- story books for page turning
- broad paintbrushes for mark making.

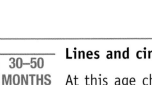

30–50 MONTHS

Lines and circles

At this age children's fine motor skills are becoming increasingly sophisticated, for example they will begin to hold a pencil between their thumb and two fingers, use it with increasing control and copy some familiar letters. But they will also use their gross motor skills to draw lines and circles.

You can combine developing children's mark-making skills with moving their whole bodies in a number of different ways by providing chalk outside alongside everyday equipment. Suggest that children use the chalk to make marks (lines and circles) to show where they've been. The observation in the Development matters! feature below shows how this activity might be carried out.

Extension idea: You may like to set out a simple obstacle course for children to follow and record in chalk, allowing for different types of movement, such as sliding down the slide, crawling through tunnels, passing through hoops, throwing a bean bag at a target.

Development matters!

A unique child: observing what children are learning

Below is an excerpt from a free description child observation which records a 3-year-old child participating in the lines and circles activity (described above) in the playground of a pre-school.

Practitioner: There are lots of things to do outside today. And I thought it would be fun to give each of you some chalk. You can use your chalk to make some lines and circles that will show where you've been and what you've played with. Shall I show you? First, I think I'll go and have a go on the slide.

The practitioner bends down and makes a chalk line on the ground en route to the slide.

Practitioner: And I'm making a chalk line to show where I've been.

She pretends to have a go on the slide.

Practitioner: Now I'm going to draw a circle around the slide to show that I played on it. Next I'm going over to the climbing frame, so I'm going to draw another line as I go ... and what do you think I'll do to show that I played on the climbing frame?

Child: Draw a circle around it?

Practitioner: That's right! Would you like some chalk?

Child: Yellow!

Child takes yellow chalk from packet.

Practitioner: And what do you think you'll play on today?

Child: Everything! I'm going to make lots and lots of circles and lines. All over.

Practitioner: And how will we know which are your lines and circles and which are mine?

Child: Don't know.

Practitioner: What colour is my chalk?

Child: Pink. (Pause) But my chalk is yellow.

Practitioner: That's right. So the pink lines and circles will show where I've been, and the yellow ones will show where you've been.

Child bends down and carefully draws a line en route to the tunnel ...

Development matters!

Enabling environments: what adults could provide

Resources and activities within early years settings that help to promote development of gross motor skills from 2 to 4 years include:

- ball games involving the passing and receiving of balls of varying sizes through catching, bouncing, rolling and kicking

- hoopla with rings, and other target games – throwing beanbags into hoops
- walking along broad balancing beams
- jumping across stepping stones drawn on the playground with chalk
- crawling and wriggling through tunnels
- going for walks
- running games such as catch, and musical bumps for starting and stopping
- swinging and sliding on medium-sized items of playground equipment
- jumping, hopping, skipping, changing-direction games (You can play while singing the following rhyme: 'I went to school one morning and I hopped like this, I hopped like this, I hopped like this, I went to school one morning and I hopped like this, all on my way to school!' Children do the hopping action throughout, then choose a new one, jumping perhaps, and so the rhyme continues.)
- circle games, such as 'The farmer's in his den', 'Here we go round the mulberry bush'
- ride-on toys with pedals, including tricycles
- twirling streamers
- learning to swim.

Development matters!

Enabling environments: what adults could provide

Resources that help to promote development of fine motor skills and hand–eye coordination for 3- to 4-year-olds include:

- scissors for cutting
- beakers with one handle to promote single-handed drinking
- simple puzzles for manipulating shapes that fit together

- dressing-up clothes for dressing and doing up simple fastenings, such as buttons, zips, Velcro
- a stocked cooking station for cooking activities involving stirring
- a sand tray and spades for digging
- a water tray and jugs for pouring
- fine items for making collages, such as string, wool, tissue
- pencils, pens and paper for drawing simple pictures
- medium-sized paintbrushes for mark making and new painting resources, such as paint rollers, to explore
- a train set for manipulating the train around the track
- play dough and other malleable materials for manipulation.

Figure 3.6 At this stage, children are beginning to cut with scissors

Guide to the learning and development requirements

Group collage

At this age, children benefit from activities that enable them to practise manipulation and the skills needed to use a range of tools and materials successfully. Two popular activities are:

- making collages – children stick relatively small items, such as paper shapes or sequins, onto their own piece of paper or card
- making recycled models – children stick recycled items together, such as yoghurt pots, cardboard packets and tubes, to make a model.

Why not try combining these activities to create a large-scale piece of collage work that the whole group can collaborate on? This can create a busy, creative environment that encourages children to become inspired by one another and to try new ways of handling both materials and tools. The activity can be done inside or outside.

- You'll need a very large sheet of strong paper (it is ideal to cut a piece from a roll of sugar paper) and a wide variety of interesting items to stick on.
- As the children will be working on a large scale, you can provide bigger materials (usually used for recycling models) for them to stick onto the large piece of paper as part of the collage. You can also give children the opportunity to handle larger quantities of materials than they may be used to – whole lengths of crepe paper, fabric or wool for example. Try to include some natural materials, such as fir cones, shells or craft feathers too.
- Make sure there are plenty of tools and a range of sticking resources on hand, such as scissors, hole punches, ink stamps, glue pens, PVA glue, spreaders and sticky tape.
- Adults should be on hand to help when necessary, particularly with the items that children wish to stick

down with sticky tape as this can be a fiddly task. (Tip – you could try using masking tape instead of sticky tape. In addition to being stronger, masking tape can be painted over later if required.)

❗ Don't forget

Teach children why it's important to use tools safely and how this is done in practice. There should be sensible rules in place.

Development matters!

Enabling environments: what adults could provide

Resources and activities within early years settings that help to promote development of gross motor skills from 5 years upwards include:

- trampolines – with close supervision, and only one child on the trampoline at a time
- running races
- bat and ball games – with various types of bat and racket
- ball games – football, basketball, netball, volleyball
- twirling batons
- frisbee games
- a range of playground games with running, chasing, dodging
- skipping-rope group games and skipping alone
- riding bicycles
- climbing, sliding and swinging on larger equipment.

Resources that help to promote development of fine motor skills and hand–eye coordination of children aged 4 years include:

- scissors for cutting out along lines and around large shapes
- knives and forks for feeding self, using both hands
- computers for use of a keyboard and mouse
- puzzles of around 12 to 20 pieces for manipulating shapes that fit together
- dressing-up clothes for doing up finer fastenings: buttons, zips, poppers, buckles etc.
- a stocked cooking station and/or malleable materials (such as play dough, Plasticine) with tools for rolling, cutting and shaping
- a range of painting resources for stamping, rollering and printing
- finer mark-making materials, such as pens and pencils for drawing more sophisticated and recognisable pictures and patterns
- access to mark-making materials during playful activities, such as role play, for emergent writing that resembles real letters and numbers
- finer craft materials, such as sequins and confetti for collage making.

Resources that help to promote development of fine motor skills and hand–eye coordination of children aged 5 years include:

- coloured pencils/felt-tips for colouring in own pictures
- stencils and templates for using a steady hand
- scissors for cutting items, such as thread, and cutting out pictures from magazines
- puzzles of over 20 pieces for manipulating shapes that fit together
- access to a stocked food preparation area for spreading bread with butter and other spreads
- small hand-held electronic toys for manipulating buttons.

Health and self-care

There are many factors that contribute to the overall health and well-being of children, and if there are difficulties with any of these factors, the effects can be detrimental to children's physical development.

Diet

In order to grow, develop and be healthy, children need a balanced diet which includes plenty of fruit and vegetables. Learning to make healthy food choices begins in the early years.

Rest and sleep

Rest and sleep are important for all humans, whatever their age. A good balance of restful, quiet activities and adequate stimulation is needed throughout the day, alongside sufficient night-time sleep and, if required, daytime naps. Not getting enough sleep – known as 'sleep deprivation' – can have a far-reaching effect. This is because sleep fulfils so many functions when the right amount is received.

Neural connections are made in the brain while children sleep. Sleep aids the brain to process information, and also aids concentration and memory function. It also seems to contribute to the formation of memories. Sleep supports a healthy immune system and the repair of damage to the body's cells – tissue damage to skin caused by UV light, for example, can be supported via sleep. In children, human growth hormone is released during a deep sleep, and a chronic lack of sleep can affect this hormone release and thereby disrupt growth patterns.

Lack of sleep/rest can lead to lethargy, irritability and emotional outbursts. Children who are suffering from lack of sleep are less able to control their behaviour and their impulses. Reduced immunity can lead to frequent colds and infections, and can increase the risk of becoming overweight. Concentration and memory are affected by a lack of sleep, and creativity and problem-solving skills can be reduced. All of these have a detrimental effect on learning and development.

Stimulation

Children need stimulation in order for their brains and bodies to develop and for learning to take place. Free play, activities, experiences, and interactions with adults and other children can all provide stimulation through action and movement.

Physical activity and exercise

Physical activity and exercise is essential for all humans. It helps to keep the heart healthy, and strengthens the lungs, muscles and bones. It simultaneously helps children to learn and consolidate physical skills.

Supporting independence in self-care

Most children will eventually take care of their bodies independently. The skills required to do this are learned gradually. When attending to a child's care needs, practitioners can:

- show children how to carry out tasks, such as washing, dressing and cleaning their teeth

- encourage children to help the adult as they are washed, dressed and so on. The extent of help will depend on the child's age and ability

- encourage children to take care of the environment as they care for themselves by keeping areas tidy and safe – for example, by avoiding or cleaning up spillages of water in the bathroom

- praise children for their attempts at self-care

- have high expectations of what children can achieve whilst ensuring they are properly supported.

◉ Early learning goal

Health and self-care: Children know the importance for good health of physical exercise, and a healthy diet, and talk about ways to keep healthy and safe. They manage their own basic hygiene and personal needs successfully, including dressing and going to the toilet independently.

Activity ideas

BIRTH–20 MONTHS

Feeding

Babies and young children in this age range are learning to respond to the emotional and physical care given to them by their carers. They're also learning to express their own needs and feelings, such as hunger, thirst, tiredness, pain and discomfort. It's important for practitioners to recognise these needs and feelings, and to respond to them appropriately and in line with the wishes of the child's parents.

At this stage, allow babies and young children to share control over their food and drink. For example, let a baby wrap their fingers around yours as you feed them their bottle of milk. If they are able to hold their own bottle or cup, support them to do so. When they are ready to move on to feeding themselves, give them finger foods and encourage attempts to feed themselves with a spoon. At this stage it is helpful to support a child by having two spoons – one for them to use and one for you to feed them with in between their own attempts. This helps to avoid the child becoming frustrated with their own efforts as much of the food is likely to fall off the spoon at first.

❗ Don't forget

Cultural attitudes towards the following may vary:

- independence
- feeding/eating
- toileting
- bathing/self-care.

Practitioners should discuss expectations with families and respect their views.

ACTIVITY IDEA

16–26 MONTHS

Dressing and self-care

At this age, children are increasingly able to help with dressing and undressing, and also with routine care tasks such as washing and brushing their hair. Not only is this important for their future independence, but it also impacts on their confidence and self-esteem.

Most young children show a desire to help with these tasks, at least some of the time! In addition, there are often occasions when young children would like to do something entirely by themselves they cannot yet manage effectively, such as washing their hands when they are covered in paint, or brushing their own teeth. Carers need to be sensitive in terms of striking the right balance between carrying out a task for a child and supporting them to do it themselves.

Allow plenty of time for dressing and care routines so that you can give children the time and patience they need to be an active participant. Praise their efforts to help however small, such as lifting up their leg so you can put their sock on. Try to break tasks down and encourage children to do what they can – for instance, encourage a child who cannot yet put on their own coat to go and fetch their coat by themselves instead, or assist a child who cannot put on their pants or trousers by themselves by putting their legs into the tricky leg holes so that they can then pull them up unaided.

For tasks children would prefer to do alone but aren't yet able to, let them try by themselves and praise their efforts, then step in to help them 'finish off'. This ensures important tasks such as hand washing are carried out hygienically, with the child's self-esteem and confidence in their own abilities intact.

Extension idea: As children move into the next age band, you can continue to promote these skills by offering opportunities to put clothes on and take them off, and manage various fastenings. Dressing-up clothes and putting clothes on dolls and soft toys are also good options. Children enjoy role play related to self-care, such as bathing the dolls in the water tray, or cooking and perhaps even feeding one another in the home corner.

Development matters!

A unique child: observing what children are learning

Below is an excerpt from a free description child observation which records a 2½-year-old child, Milo, helping his key worker, Sally, to get him dressed after he has been playing in a paddling pool.

Milo stands in front of Sally, who is kneeling on the floor. She holds out Milo's pants for him. He puts his hands on Sally's shoulders to steady himself and steps into them. Sally pulls them part of the way up, then waits while Milo pulls them up the rest of the way himself. When Milo sees Sally pick up his shorts, he puts his hands on her shoulders once again and the previous actions are completed. Next, Sally picks up Milo's T-shirt. He leans forward and puts his head inside, then starts to scramble about inside, trying to find the armholes. Sally reaches through each armhole in turn and guides his hands out.

Sally asks Milo to fetch his shoes from the shoe rack. He does this and brings them back to Sally. He takes his socks out of his shoes and hands them to her. He sits down and lifts each leg in turn so that Sally can put on his socks and then his shoes. His shoes have a Velcro fastening and Sally encourages Milo to fasten his shoes himself.

Development matters!

Positive relationships: what adults could do

Katharina is a childminder working with 2-year-old Billy. He has been painting, but now it's time to get ready for lunch. Billy enjoys doing things for himself, and generally washes his hands independently. But after doing so today, he's still covered in paint. Katharina points this out, and asks Billy if he'd like some help to get the remaining paint off. Billy refuses, so Katharina patiently directs him back to the sink and supports him verbally instead. She praises the effort he's making, 'Well done, there's lots of paint going down the plug hole now, isn't there?' and also helps him to complete the task to a hygienic standard, 'Do you think you could rub some soap on the paint on your thumb? That's it ...'

Healthy picnic

ACTIVITY IDEA

22–36 MONTHS

At this stage, children are quite independent in feeding themselves competently. They also begin to be able to think and talk about the food they like or dislike, and often enjoy helping with simple food preparation, such as peeling a banana. So this is an ideal time to give children positive messages about healthy food choices.

One way to do this is to involve children in preparing and packing up a 'healthy picnic'. This can be as simple as snacks that will be enjoyed in the garden, or it could be a meal to be shared on an outing to somewhere such as the local park. Whilst packing up the picnic, encourage conversation with the children about the foods selected and talk about how they are prepared. When eating the picnic, talk about the taste and textures of the food they are eating. The picnic element helps to create special interest. By referring to the container as a 'healthy picnic basket' you will help cement in children's minds the idea that certain foods are healthy. Having a picnic is fun, which is of course a vital ingredient!

Figure 3.7 Involve children in the preparation of food

> ## ❶ *Don't forget*
>
> Learning to go to the toilet independently is an important part of self-care. Bowel and bladder control develops at different times in different children. It often occurs between the age of about 18 months and 3 years. Most children are dry and clean during the daytime by the time they are 3. Night-time control takes longer to develop. Many children still have accidents at night until the age of 6 or 7, and some beyond this age. Some children with disabilities or special educational needs may develop bowel and bladder control much later, and may continue to use nappies. Some may never develop control.

30–50 MONTHS

Rest and lively play

At this stage, a child can communicate to adults when they want to rest or engage in lively play – but to do this effectively they need to understand what their body is telling them.

You can help children to recognise the changes that occur in their bodies when they rest and play, and to understand why it's important to do both every day to stay healthy. It's particularly helpful for children to appreciate why they should rest when they feel tired, as they are then less likely to fight tiredness and 'go until they drop'. (The planning excerpt in the Development matters! feature on page 99 gives examples of activities which promote this through a 'My body' theme.)

It is important to foster a love of lively, energetic play in the early years as physical activity is key to maintaining good health throughout life. Why not try the following games:
- Traffic lights
- What's the time, Mr Wolf?
- Musical bumps
- Parachute games
- Simon says
- Captain's coming.

These childhood favourites are familiar to many, but for details of how to play these and many other lively games you can visit the following websites:
- www.playgroundfun.org.uk
- www.gameskidsplay.net
- www.teachingexpertise.com (and then type 'traditional playground games' into the search box)
- http://spoonful.com (and then click on 'play')
- www.activityvillage.co.uk
- http://guidinguk.freeservers.com (and then click on 'contents', 'games and activities' and 'parachute games')
- www.funandgames.org (and then click on 'games directory').

Take care to only select games suitable for the age of the children with whom you work. Remember to consider any individual needs children may have and to make adaptations where necessary to enable everyone to participate. For example, the group may play parachute games kneeling up as opposed to standing so a child who uses a wheelchair can participate fully.

The lists of resources and activities to support gross motor skill development given in the Development matters! features on pages 84–85 and on page 88 are also helpful in providing energetic play opportunities.

Toiletries that care for our bodies

40–60 MONTHS

You will need:
- Story books about going on holiday, such as *Rosie's Holiday*, *Spot Goes on Holiday*
- A person puppet (you can use a doll or other alternative if preferred)
- A suitcase with a few puppet- or doll-sized clothes and an empty toiletry bag packed inside
- Pencils and paper
- Spare toiletry bags
- Imaginary area set up as a shop/chemist and stocked with toiletries to buy

What to do:
- Share the stories about going on holiday with children.
- Talk about packing for a holiday – ask children open-ended questions, such as 'What do people usually take with them?' 'What do they pack their things in?' Direct discussion around to the things people take so they can look after their bodies while they are away: toothbrush and paste, a hairbrush, a sponge, shower gel or bubble bath, soap, shampoo etc.
- Introduce the children to a person puppet, and explain that they are visiting your city/town/village on holiday. They've just arrived and it's time for them to unpack.
- Open the puppet's suitcase and talk about the clothes inside. Now

open the toiletry bag, and make the 'discovery' that it's empty – 'Oh no! There's nothing inside! She's forgotten all of the things she needs to care for her body while she's on her holiday! What can we do to help?' Direct conversation around to the solution of buying everything the puppet needs from a shop.

- Using the children's suggestions, write a shopping list of items needed to go into the toiletry bag then, together, take the puppet shopping in the imaginary area. Check off the items on the list as they are found.
- Once the shopping has been paid for, the children can pack the toiletry bag.
- Encourage the children to now play freely in the imaginary area. Make pencils and paper available for writing their own shopping lists, and spare toiletry bags available for packing when they've made their purchases.

Development matters!

Enabling environments: what adults could provide

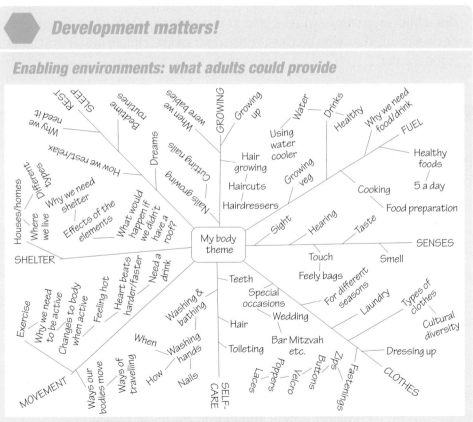

Figure 3.8 Excerpt from 'My body' theme-planning

Development matters!

Positive relationships: what adults could do

After a lively game outside, children's centre practitioner, Camille, asks the children to sit in a small circle. She talks to them about how their bodies feel after running around. She shows them how to put their hands on their chest and feel their hearts beating faster, and encourages them to listen to their rapid breathing.

She asks the children how their bodies feel. One child says, 'Hot'. Camille says, 'Where do you feel hot?' The child says, 'My face'. Camille encourages all the children to touch their cheeks and foreheads, and to notice if they too feel hot. Camille asks them what they can do to cool down a little bit. The group decide it will be helpful to open a window and let in some fresh air. They also decide to take off any outer layers of clothing, such as jumpers and cardigans.

One child says she is thirsty, and several others agree. The group decide to all fill their beakers with some fresh, chilled water from the water cooler.

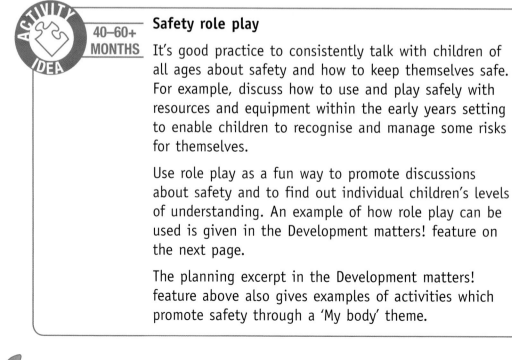

40–60+ MONTHS

Safety role play

It's good practice to consistently talk with children of all ages about safety and how to keep themselves safe. For example, discuss how to use and play safely with resources and equipment within the early years setting to enable children to recognise and manage some risks for themselves.

Use role play as a fun way to promote discussions about safety and to find out individual children's levels of understanding. An example of how role play can be used is given in the Development matters! feature on the next page.

The planning excerpt in the Development matters! feature above also gives examples of activities which promote safety through a 'My body' theme.

Positive relationships: what adults could do

Practitioner Enso is working with a group of 4- to 5-year-olds at a pre-school today. He has planned a safety-themed role play using the setting's large puppet, which the children call Charlie. The puppet is almost child sized, and Enso can put his hands right inside the sleeves and operate the arms and hands.

Enso tells the children that Charlie is new to pre-school. As it's his very first day, he doesn't know about the things he should and shouldn't do to stay safe and healthy. As Charlie 'joins in' with various activities throughout the session, Enso asks the children direct safety questions that Charlie needs to know the answers to, and also uses statements to provoke a response. For example, Enso says, 'Charlie hasn't played on the climbing frame before. Is there anything he needs to know to play safely?' One of the children replies, 'You can't take toys on the climbing frame with you'. Enso asks, 'Why is that?' The child doesn't seem sure. Her friend says, 'It's because you won't be able to hold on properly if you've got something in your hands'. The first child says, 'Yes, and you might fall off and hurt yourself'.

Later, Enso says, 'Charlie hasn't been playing with anything messy, so he doesn't think he needs to wash his hands before snack time ...' One child replies, 'He always has to'. Another says, 'You can't see germs'.

⬤ Personal, social and emotional development

According to the EYFS framework, personal, social and emotional development involves helping children to:

- develop a positive sense of themselves and form positive relationships
- develop social skills and learn how to manage their feelings
- understand appropriate behaviour in groups
- have confidence in their own abilities.

Why is personal, social and emotional development a prime area of learning?

Personal, social and emotional development underpins much of children's overall learning and development. It focuses on the way in which children experience and handle their own emotions, which gives rise to how they then behave – frustration at not being able to do something is a good example of this. Children gain increasing control of their emotions as they develop.

This area is also concerned with children's attachments to key people in their lives and their relationships with others, including how they relate to them. This has strong links to communication and language development, as communication and understanding is at the heart of all relationships, as is the act of expressing feelings and emotions.

Another important aspect of personal, social and emotional development is learning about morality – or, in other words, learning about the values and principles that inform what is considered to be socially acceptable behaviour in our society (for example, that physically hurting others is wrong). This requires the development of emotional control as well as knowledge. For instance, a child may know that it is wrong to hit someone, but knowing how to control anger and behaviour so as not to do so is another matter.

In short, the way children are feeling, behaving and relating towards others will constantly influence the things they do, the way they do them, what and who they engage with, the quality of their relationships and, often what they ultimately achieve.

Figure 3.9 Children gain increasing control of their emotions as they develop

Guide to the learning and development requirements

The ELGs

There are three ELGs for this prime area of learning:

1. Self-confidence and self-awareness (see below)

2. Managing feelings and behaviour (see page 110)

3. Making relationships (see page 118).

Each one is explained in detail in the relevant section that follows.

Self-confidence and self-awareness

> ### ◉ Early learning goal
>
> **Self-confidence and self-awareness**: Children are confident to try new activities, and say why they like some activities more than others. They are confident to speak in a familiar group, will talk about their ideas, and will choose the resources they need for their chosen activities. They say when they do or don't need help.

Activity ideas

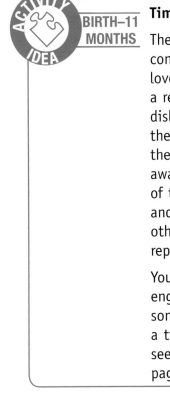

BIRTH–11 MONTHS

Time together

The most important things you can do to promote self-confidence for the youngest age range is to show them love, warmth and affection and to interact with them in a responsive, sensitive way that respects their likes and dislikes. Positive one-to-one interactions are key – see the activity on 'Early conversations' on page 66. Through these you can also help babies develop a sense of self-awareness, as they will learn that they can use aspects of themselves – their voice, gestures, facial expressions and eye contact – to connect and communicate with others. Your sensitive response will cause babies to repeat their actions.

You can also help babies to develop self-awareness by engaging in pleasurable physical interactions, such as songs like 'Round and round the garden' which ends in a tickle, moving a baby's body to a beat or rhythm – see the activities on 'Tones' and 'Moving to the beat' on pages 54 and 55.

8–20 MONTHS

Sense of self

Babies and young children are now increasingly developing a sense of self, and you can provide activities that help babies to recognise that they are separate and different to others. For example, you can playfully point to or touch parts of their body and help them to learn their names. Try playing a game of 'Where's your nose?' for example (see the Development matters! feature below) as young children in this age range enjoy this.

Mirrors help babies to understand who they are. You can enhance this by looking in the mirror with them sometimes, so they can see the two of you reflected, and see that you are different and separate. You should also talk to them about what they see.

Children are also beginning to get a sense of their own preferences, likes and dislikes. You should therefore give them appropriate choices, such as a choice of finger foods at snack time, a choice of what toy to play with or book to look at, or how and when to explore their environment – see also the activity 'Treasure baskets' on page 121.

Young children will increasingly be able to communicate their wants and needs, for example by beginning to point at objects of desire and actively looking to you for help.

Development matters!

A unique child: observing what children are learning

Excerpt from a free description observation of an 18-month-old child in which a practitioner uses a naturally occurring opportunity to explore and extend the child's sense of self.

Callum sits on the lap of his key worker, Skyler. He has come for some love and attention and is in a playful mood. He touches the clip in Skyler's hair which is in the shape of a butterfly. Skyler says, 'There's a pretty butterfly in my hair today ... Where's Callum's hair?' Callum touches his head with his whole hand. Skyler says, 'That's right ... and where's Callum's nose?' Callum touches his nose with one finger. He then touches Skyler's nose. She says, 'That's Skyler's nose, isn't it? And where are my ears?' Callum touches his left ear. 'That's your ear, isn't it? Callum's ear. Where's Skyler's ear?' Callum touches Skyler's left ear. 'Well done, that's Skyler's ear.' Skyler touches Callum's left ear and then his right. 'And here are Callum's ears, one, two ...'

ACTIVITY IDEA

16–26 MONTHS

Making choices

In this age band, children are increasingly keen to do some things independently, which demonstrates that their sense of self is becoming more sophisticated. This is very plain to see when a child begins to tell adults 'no'. However, this will lead to some frustration as children will not always be able to manage all the things they would like to do themselves. Provide support, patience and plenty of activities that allow young children to make decisions for themselves and take the lead in their own play. Provide opportunities for pretend play to allow children to do the things they would like to in their own imaginary worlds.

Children are just starting to pretend so you need to provide sensitive support and access to imaginary resources that represent the everyday world around them – see the activity 'Imagine this' on page 192.

❶ *Don't forget*

You should always remember to work inclusively, so make sure there are enabling choices available for all children in your care.

Development matters!

Ranek is the supervisor of a brand new day nursery that will be opening in a few months' time. She's currently planning the layout of each room and ordering resources and furniture.

While adults will set up particular and varied activities and resources throughout each day, Ranek is keen to make additional resources available for children to access independently, such as toys and books, and materials such as paper and tools for mark making. This will ensure that they have plenty of opportunity to choose and lead their own play and experiences.

She decides to order shelving units of varying heights for each room. They are made especially to house a number of plastic storage boxes, which come in various sizes. Ranek plans to make picture labels for each of the boxes and stick them on, so children can select what they want without having to go through lots of boxes. They will also be able to see where to put things away at tidy-up time. In the rooms for older children, Ranek will add a word label to each box, such as 'trains'.

Development matters!

Positive relationships: what adults could do

Once Ranek has organised the layout of each of the rooms at the new day nursery to enable children to access the resources independently, it will be important to teach the children to use and care for the resources provided and then trust them to do so independently. She makes a mental note to convey this to the staff. All the resources are new, lovely and have cost a lot of money, but they are there to be well used.

Next on Ranek's to-do list is to check that she has ordered sufficient resources to reflect the cultural diversity of society. (See pages 168–170 for some suggested resources that reflect cultural diversity.)

Jobs board

30–50 MONTHS

Children enjoy the responsibility of carrying out small tasks. A jobs board lists a number of daily tasks and allows you to assign them to different children each day. Looking at the board with the group at a familiar time each day (such as circle time) helps to highlight the importance of different job roles, and allows children to see that there is a clear and fair rota system that ensures everyone gets their turn.

Names displayed on the jobs board also serve as a prompt for adults to ask children about their special task, and to praise them for what they have done. When talking about who will do each job today, you can mention which adult will be with the children. This helps children to see adults as a resource, and to have confidence in asking adults for help.

You will need:
- A notice board – a cork board you have purchased or, if you prefer, you can make your own
- Cardboard strips
- A marker pen
- Velcro adhesive pads
- Scissors

What to do:

Write all the children's names on individual cardboard strips, trimmed to the appropriate size. You may wish to have these laminated for durability, in which case you will need to round off sharp corners with scissors.

Repeat step one, except this time write out each individual job. Jobs might include feeding the nursery pet, watering the plants, fetching the post from the setting's mailbox, taking the register to the office, setting the table.

Make a heading on a cardboard strip, such as 'Our jobs'.

Fix Velcro adhesive pads to the back of each of the strips. The heading will go in the top centre of the board, and the jobs will go in a list on the left-hand side. Fix the corresponding pieces of Velcro in the right places on the board, and stick the heading and jobs in place.

Each day, children's names will be placed opposite each of the jobs on the right-hand side of the board, so fix the corresponding pieces of Velcro in the right places to facilitate this.

Hang the board on the wall.

Extension idea: It's a good idea to make the board more meaningful to children by adding a visual image for each job. This could be a simple picture of a watering can, for instance, or you could take a photo of a child undertaking each task.

Development matters!

Positive relationships: what adults could do

Understanding choices made

The following example shows how children need to learn that the choices they make may mean that they can't do something else.

Sebastian is a childminder. He cares for Talia, who will be 3 in three weeks' time. Today they've been on a special outing to a nearby adventure park. They've had an exciting day seeing farm animals and exploring playgrounds, soft play and park areas developed especially for the under 5s.

As Talia had been looking forward to the special trip for some time, her mum decided to give her some money to spend on an ice cream and something from the gift shop. Talia bought her ice cream earlier on.

As they enter the shop, Sebastian reminds Talia that she has £3.50 to spend and she will need to choose something she can afford. Talia's attention is immediately grabbed by some large soft toy farm animals. Sebastian agrees that they are lovely and says, 'They cost quite a bit more than £3.50 though, so shall we keep looking around?' Talia spots several other expensive items and Sebastian senses she is getting frustrated with his repetitive answer. He steers Talia towards a display of toys that are in the right price range and says, 'There are some lovely toys here that you could buy with your money, Talia.'

Talia has a good look. She decides that she likes a small, soft toy goat, and she also likes a small world horse and foal. Sebastian explains to her that she can't afford them all. If she buys the goat she won't be able to afford anything else as all her money will be spent. If she buys the horse and foal she will have a few pennies change to put in her moneybox at home, but she won't be able to afford the goat. Talia is reluctant to choose – she really wants them all. Sebastian patiently reinforces that this isn't possible. He talks to her about why she likes each option. She talks most enthusiastically about the soft toy goat because it reminds her of her excitement at feeding a young goat earlier in the day. Sebastian suggests it would be nice to buy and look after the goat ... Talia agrees and the horse and foal are returned to the shelf.

As they leave the gift shop, Talia says she wants to go back and buy the horse and foal with her change. Sebastian reiterates that she hasn't got enough money left. Talia is frustrated and begins to whine. Sebastian sympathises but his message remains clear. He says, 'I know you liked the horse and foal, but you couldn't afford everything, so you chose the goat, didn't you? That means you can't have the horse and foal today.' He then distracts her by saying, 'We can show Mummy the goat when she picks you up, and tell her all about you feeding that hungry one earlier. What else can we tell her about today?'

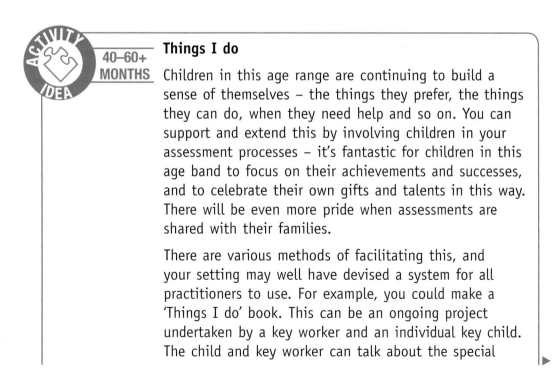

40–60+ MONTHS

Things I do

Children in this age range are continuing to build a sense of themselves – the things they prefer, the things they can do, when they need help and so on. You can support and extend this by involving children in your assessment processes – it's fantastic for children in this age band to focus on their achievements and successes, and to celebrate their own gifts and talents in this way. There will be even more pride when assessments are shared with their families.

There are various methods of facilitating this, and your setting may well have devised a system for all practitioners to use. For example, you could make a 'Things I do' book. This can be an ongoing project undertaken by a key worker and an individual key child. The child and key worker can talk about the special things that make the child who they are, and find ways to represent them in the book, such as through a range of photographs, artwork by the child, other images and summary sentences. For example, the book may include:

- images of the child's favourite places with a sentence about why they like it or what they do there
- information about their preferred activities and special toys
- details of children's recent new experiences and skills they have mastered or are learning
- information about a child's interests, the things they do with their families
- details about important relationships in their lives, including special friends.

Within each area, you should try to draw children's attention to the things that are their own special qualities and opinions. For example, you may talk about and list 'Ways that I am a friend' (sharing, playing together, being kind when someone is upset etc.) or 'Ways that I have fun'.

❗ Don't forget

It's important to continue to provide children with activities that are challenging but achievable. This not only promotes learning and development in terms of skills, it gives children a sense of self-confidence and achievement.

Managing feelings and behaviour

◉ Early learning goal

Managing feelings and behaviour: Children talk about how they and others show feelings, talk about their own and others' behaviour and its consequences, and know that some behaviour is unacceptable. They work as part of a group or class, and understand and follow the rules. They adjust their behaviour to different situations, and take changes of routine in their stride.

Activity ideas

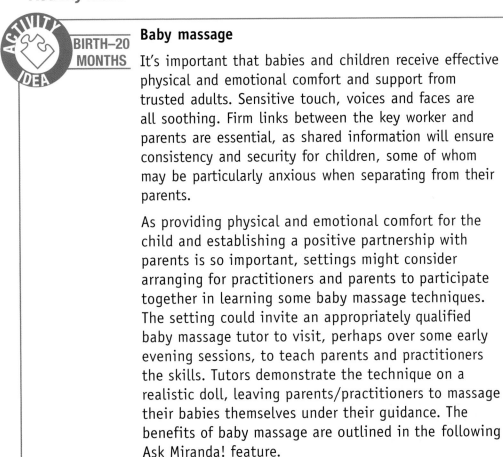

ACTIVITY IDEA

BIRTH–20 MONTHS

Baby massage

It's important that babies and children receive effective physical and emotional comfort and support from trusted adults. Sensitive touch, voices and faces are all soothing. Firm links between the key worker and parents are essential, as shared information will ensure consistency and security for children, some of whom may be particularly anxious when separating from their parents.

As providing physical and emotional comfort for the child and establishing a positive partnership with parents is so important, settings might consider arranging for practitioners and parents to participate together in learning some baby massage techniques. The setting could invite an appropriately qualified baby massage tutor to visit, perhaps over some early evening sessions, to teach parents and practitioners the skills. Tutors demonstrate the technique on a realistic doll, leaving parents/practitioners to massage their babies themselves under their guidance. The benefits of baby massage are outlined in the following Ask Miranda! feature.

---

❶ Don't forget

You should not massage babies unless you are trained to do so, and you should seek permission from the setting to introduce massage into the routine.

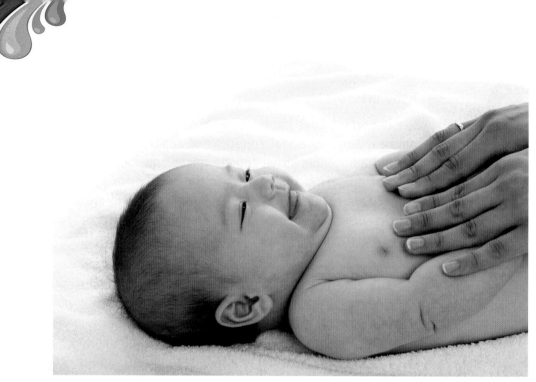

Figure 3.10 Baby massage provides emotional and physical comfort

Ask Miranda!

Q: What are the benefits of baby massage?

A: According to the Guild of Sensory Development (www.gicm.org.uk):

- Massage is an excellent way of connecting with your baby.
- A short massage can help your baby to feel loved.
- Massage can alleviate trapped wind, soothe colic or alleviate constipation.
- Massaging the jaw can relax a baby who has just begun to take solids.
- Massaging the gums through the skin may ease the pain of teething.
- A face massage can unblock a baby's blocked nose.
- Massage can alleviate the effects of post-natal depression and help a mother to have a more positive interaction with her baby.

Guide to the learning and development requirements

Benefits of baby massage for your child

- It smoothes transition from the womb to the world.
- It develops a baby's first language: touch.
- It teaches positive, loving touch.
- It develops a feeling of being loved, respected and secure.
- It develops a child's body, mind, awareness and coordination.
- It can help to reduce the discomfort of colic, wind and constipation.
- It helps to regulate and strengthen a baby's digestive and respiratory systems, and stimulate circulatory and nervous systems.
- It promotes relaxation.
- It can help to reduce 'fussiness' and improve a child's quality of sleep.
- It improves skin condition.

Benefits of baby massage for parents

- It helps parents to understand a baby's non-verbal communication.
- It enhances parents' confidence and competence in dealing with their baby.
- It can help with post-natal depression.
- Both parents and baby relax together.
- It promotes lactation in breastfeeding mothers (through the stimulation of hormones).
- It promotes the nurturing instinct (through stimulation of the hormone oxytocin).

16–26 MONTHS

Learning to share

Children are now learning that some things are theirs, some things are shared and some things belong to other people. This can be a difficult, frustrating thing ▶

both to learn and accept. A desire to have something can be a strong emotion for all of us, and children are often overwhelmed by it, leading to frustration and possibly a tantrum when thwarted.

Help children to learn to share, but expectations must be realistic so make sure that there are duplicates of some materials and resources to reduce conflict. It's unreasonable to expect young children to share all of the time! Seek out some books for this age range that illustrate cooperative behaviour, such as sharing and turn taking, and talk about the feelings of the characters depicted. This is quite a common theme in books for this age range.

Also, why not take some photos of individual children with their own things, such as a special toy or a blanket, and then some photos of them sharing various resources within the setting? These can then be made into a wall display, which can become a visual reminder and a discussion point. When it's time for the display to come down, you can reuse the components to make a book for children to handle.

Feelings

22–50 MONTHS

Children are now increasingly aware and able to talk about their own feelings, and they know that some actions and thoughts can hurt the feelings of others. At this stage, encourage children to talk a lot about feelings. Help them to understand that all feelings are acceptable, but that not all behaviours are – for instance, it is acceptable to feel angry but unacceptable to harm someone else.

Refer to the activity on 'Persona resources' and the Development matters! feature on page 164 for suggested activities.

Development matters!

Positive relationships: what adults could do

Two 4-year-olds, Caleb and Gracie, are playing in the imaginary corner. Caleb is wearing the police hat from the dressing-up box. Gracie also wants to wear it, and she's trying to take it from Caleb's head. Caleb is protesting loudly and hanging on to it.

(This is a familiar scene in any setting. By the time they are 4, most children will have had plenty of experience of an adult settling this type of dispute for them and are likely to know how this is done.)

Practitioner Lindsey intervenes. She asks the children what's wrong. Both say they want to wear the hat. Lindsey says, 'I see, there's only one police hat, and Caleb's wearing it at the moment. So what can we do?' Caleb suggests that Gracie has it next. Lindsey says, 'That sounds like a good idea. What do you think Gracie?' Gracie agrees. Lindsey says, 'So what can Gracie do while she's waiting?' Gracie suggests that she could wear a different hat. Caleb goes to the dressing-up box to help her find one.

Codes of behaviour

40–60+ MONTHS

Boundaries set appropriate limits for children's behaviour and help children to learn how to behave in safe and acceptable ways. What children know and understand about boundaries will depend on their age, abilities and experience. The younger children in this age range may just be starting to learn about boundaries through repetition – they will need to be reminded of boundaries frequently. Children of school age are likely to have a good understanding of them.

Try to involve the children in establishing a simple set of ground rules. This helps children to accept the boundaries and appreciate their purpose. The ground rules must reflect the behaviour policy of the setting.

▶

What to do:

1. Involve the children in establishing a set of ground rules by encouraging discussion about:
    *   the ways in which children want to be treated by others
    *   the types of behaviour and actions that:
        - contribute to a pleasant, positive environment
        - contribute to an unpleasant, negative environment
        - hurt other people emotionally and physically
        - help to avoid confrontation and to handle disagreements and conflict positively
        - help to keep everyone safe and healthy.

2. Write down the rules, making sure that they are phrased using positive language – 'Be kind to other people', is much better than, 'No hitting, scratching, kicking, biting ...' etc.

3. You can then have a discussion about what does and doesn't constitute kind behaviour, as necessary. The final set of ground rules is likely to focus on:
    *   showing respect for others
    *   getting along with peers
    *   having a positive attitude
    *   using acceptable language
    *   not hurting others physically or emotionally
    *   following safety and health requirements.

---

❶ Don't forget

It is up to practitioners to help children understand boundaries whilst communicating to them that the boundaries are firm. This is known as 'defining boundaries'. It needs to be done through a consistent approach. When children are about to overstep a boundary, you should take the opportunity to remind them of the boundary and why it exists, as shown in the practical example in the Development matters! feature on the next page. Children learn from this, and it is often enough to stop them in their tracks and deter them from inappropriate behaviour.

Development matters!

A unique child: observing what children are learning

Excerpt from a free narrative observation of a 4-year-old child, demonstrating the setting of boundaries.

> Chloe (C) is playing a board game with three other 3- to 4-year-olds. She throws the dice. Smiles. Says, 'Three'. She moves her counter saying, 'One, two, three'. She watches another child have a turn. She fiddles with her counters. The practitioner (P) says, 'Leave them there won't you, until your turn.' C pauses then puts out her hand to take the dice from the child whose turn it is next. P says, 'Remember that we all need to wait for our turn. That way the game is fair, and everyone has fun.' C puts her hands in her lap.

Development matters!

Positive relationships: what adults could do

Age of child	Example boundary issue	Response of practitioner
1–2 years	Children do not yet understand the dangers that exist around them and may repeatedly do something potentially dangerous.	Syed is trying to remove a safety plug socket cover from the wall. Childminder Katy has spoken to him before about this. She patiently intervenes once more. She says a firm 'no' and explains why the behaviour is unacceptable. She knows that children of this age learn through repetition and need to be shown patience.
2–3 years	Children may swing between being independent and dependent, becoming frustrated when they don't have the skills to perform the tasks they want to for themselves.	Francesca wants to put on her shoes herself. She gets them on but struggles with the buckle. Frustrated, she takes one shoe off again and throws it onto the floor. Practitioner Rob approaches and says, 'Well done Francesca, you've put a shoe on by yourself! Can I help you with the buckle, and then we'll do the other shoe together?' Rob knows children of this age need praise for trying things themselves, and that it's best to ignore frustrated behaviour if possible and offer the practical assistance needed.

Age of child	Example boundary issue	Response of practitioner
3–4 years	Now children are playing more independently with peers. They will quarrel at times and experiment with behaviour as they learn to get along with others.	Ben and Jayda are falling out at the water tray over which one of them will get to play with the water wheel. Practitioner Abbey-Leigh steps in. She knows that children of this age are still learning about relationships with peers. She encourages them to resolve their own conflict with her support by saying, 'Can you think of a way you can share the water wheel?'
4–5 years	The school transition may unsettle children, and this may affect behaviour.	Recently, 4-year-old Travis has started speaking in a somewhat babyish way to his childminder, Mandy, every now and then – but particularly at mealtimes. Travis has recently started visiting the school he will go to in September. Mandy knows that children have a lot to adjust to in their life at this time and that it's important for practitioners to be patient and to support children emotionally if they regress to behaviours they had previously given up. Mandy ignores the babytalk and answers Travis as she would usually. She doesn't expect the behaviour to last long.

Making relationships

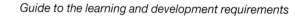 *Early learning goal*

Making relationships: Children play cooperatively, taking turns with others. They take account of one another's ideas about how to organise their activity. They show sensitivity to others' needs and feelings, and form positive relationships with adults and other children.

Guide to the learning and development requirements

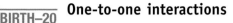

ACTIVITY IDEA

BIRTH–20 MONTHS

One-to-one interactions

Babies and young children need warm, loving relationships with key people in their lives. They need to be held and cuddled and feel that they are special to those looking after them. So it's important that practitioners plan for each child to spend some one-to-one time each session with their key worker or a buddy. Everyday care routines do provide excellent opportunities to interact with babies and give them the sense they are cared for, but one-to-one time when children are alert, responsive and willing to engage is also vital. Remember, for example, that young babies will not communicate much vocally when taking a bottle, although it is a lovely warm time for bonding and sharing affection.

Spend time playing and talking to babies and children, engage in the special games they enjoy, such as particular way of playing peek-a-boo – ask parents to share their experiences with you. You can also share stories, songs and early mimic style conversations (see the 'Early conversations' activity for Birth–11 months and the 'Responding to communications' activity for 8–20 months on pages 66–67 of the 'Communication and language' section).

❗ *Don't forget*

It's good practice for each key worker to be paired with a buddy. This is someone who also gets to know the child and their family well, so they can step into the key worker role when necessary, for instance if the key worker is on holiday, or if they should leave the employment of the setting.

Figure 3.11 Spend time engaging in special games, such as peek-a-boo

❗ Don't forget

Babies and young children are learning the ways of the world, and they need time to process the information that they receive. Remember to give babies the time they need to respond when you are interacting with them. This is often an intuitive part of a practitioner's role. It's natural to slow down your speech, to pick up the baby or child's cues, and to interact at their pace, as shown in the example in the Development matters! feature below.

⬢ Development matters!

Positive relationships: what adults could do

Nita is a childminder caring for 6-month-old Ellis. They both enjoy their lively 'conversations'. Nita sits with Ellis, and talks to him in light, playful tones. She then pauses, but maintains eye contact with him to let him know that she's still engaged with him. During the pause, Ellis has time to process what he has heard. He responds with a string of babbling sounds. Nita waits for him to finish, then she replies, and pauses once again.

Treasure baskets

At this age, children are becoming more sociable, and will play alongside their peers. They're also starting to become more independent emotionally, and will leave their carer to go and explore the environment. However, the security of the carer is as important as ever, and the child will soon return for comfort or reassurance if they feel overwhelmed or worried. Knowing that the carer is there gives the child confidence to venture away.

To promote this development, you can plan activities that encourage young children to do similar things alongside one another, while you remain a secure base to which the child can return when they want to. Heuristic play is an ideal activity for this. 'Heuristic play' is a term first used in the 1980s by child psychologist Elinor Goldschmeid to describe what happens when babies and children explore the properties of real objects (as opposed to toys). For babies and toddlers, this play centres on a 'treasure basket' filled with a diverse collection of objects, which babies can explore from the time they are able to sit up unaided.

You will need:
- Natural and manmade objects from the real world (that are appropriate for exploration by the age range you are working with), such as:
  - a whisk
  - a large pebble
  - a sponge
  - a hairbrush
  - a wooden spoon
  - a metal sieve
  - a cardboard tube
  - a square of fun fur
  - a woollen glove
- A basket or tactile container (such as a wicker box)

What to do
- Ensure the objects are clean and safe.
- Place them in the basket or container.
- Leave the basket in the centre of the floor, then move away.
- Watch from a distance as children discover the basket and explore the items.

▶

- Do not interfere unnecessarily if children are playing safely and are engaged, but remain ready to provide support or reassurance if children look for this.

Figure 3.12 Treasure baskets allow children to explore real objects alongside each other

Development matters!

Enabling environments: what adults could provide

Another way of encouraging children to become more sociable by playing alongside their peers is to provide large collections of resources that allow several children to play similarly and together if they would like to, for example a big box of balls and skittles or ride-on toys and trundle trikes.

Making time for children to greet everyone at the start of the session, and at the end of the session to say goodbye, will help children feel part of a social group. Singing 'hello' or 'goodbye' songs that feature children's names will enhance this, and help children to learn and use the names of their peers. The 'It's very nice to see you' song is ideal.

Development matters!

Parten's five stages of play

In 1932, researcher Mildred Parten was studying the play of children aged between 2 and 5 years of age. Despite her research being carried out 80 years ago, her findings are still valid today and are generally accepted. She focused on the children's social interactions during their play. Through her observations, she identified five stages of play which children pass through. You can look out for these as you complete your own observations of children aged 2 to 5 years.

Solitary play

This occurs when a child plays alone, completely independent of others. Very young children only play alone.

Spectator play

The word 'spectator' means someone who is watching. Spectator play occurs when a child watches another child or children at play but does not join in. The spectator either will not be playing themselves, or will be doing a different activity to the one they are watching. This is sometimes called 'onlooker play'. Toddlers can often be observed watching others from a distance.

Parallel play

This stage occurs from around 2 years of age. The child plays alongside others and may share resources, but they remain engrossed in their own activity. The child has companionship but, even in the middle of a group, the child remains independent in their play. They do not look at other children.

Associative play

This occurs from between the ages of 3 and 4 years. Children share resources and talk to each other. But they each have their own play agenda (own idea of what they want to do). The children don't coordinate their play objectives or interests. This means there will be some trouble! Conflicts arise when children have separate ideas that others do not share. Children especially have trouble when trying to play imaginatively together.

Cooperative play

This occurs when children fully interact, and can participate together in play with specific goals in mind. They can play their own imaginary games, organising themselves into roles etc. – 'You be the doctor and I'll be the patient ...'. The older children in Parten's study were capable of cooperative play from the ages of 4 to 5 years.

Development matters!

Enabling environments: what adults could provide

Resources/equipment to support the ELG *making relationships* can include:

- puppets, dolls and soft toys (with emotional expressions for exploring feelings)
- table-top games
- dressing-up clothes
- cultural artefacts
- a range of resources showing positive images of people, to reflect our diverse society
- well-resourced imaginary areas, including a home corner
- comfortable quiet areas for resting and talking
- space for circle time
- new activities to built confidence and motivation to join in
- activities that celebrate festivals.

Time for cooperation

22–36 MONTHS

As children are now increasingly interested in the play of others and starting to join in, it's the ideal time to introduce cooperative activities such as:

- rolling a beach ball to one another
- simple games that require turn taking – such as a basic picture lotto game
- simple games that require holding hands and moving together – such as 'Here we go round the mulberry bush', 'Ring a ring o'roses' or 'Row, row, row your boat'
- sharing spaces together that promote conversations, such as hideaway dens (see the 'post office' activity on page 140 for simple methods of creating these), a cosy book corner, an outside playhouse or a tunnel.

Children in this age band tend to cope best when cooperating in pairs or small groups.

Extension idea: Why not make your own basic lotto game using photos of the children (to make it personal and meaningful to them) for matching?

Making friends

30–50 MONTHS

Children are now increasingly able to understand the concept of friends and friendships, and will usually demonstrate friendly behaviour with peers and adults, such as starting conversations. They are now ready for more sophisticated cooperation activities and games. Why not try the following:

- 'What's the time, Mr Wolf?', a game which requires children to work as a team creeping towards the wolf together
- parachute games which require the group to move at the same time to make the parachute mushroom upwards
- the 'under and over' team game (children move a ball down the line by passing it alternatively over their

head or between their legs to the person behind them), to help children work together to achieve a task
- board games that require patience, turn taking and coping with winning and losing, such as 'The house that Jack built', 'My first snakes and ladders'.

The following activities are also useful:
- 'Persona resources' and the Development matters! feature on page 164 of this book – for using persona dolls, books and puppets to explore and understand own feelings and those of others
- 'It's a small world' and 'Imaginary areas' on pages 64–65 – for role play and expressive/imaginative play reflecting the lives of children, families and communities
- 'Everyday practices and special events' on page 171 – for broadening children's knowledge and understanding of lives that are unfamiliar (reflecting an inclusive ethos).

Circle time

40–60+ MONTHS

Children are now increasingly talking about their own knowledge, understanding and experiences, and taking account of what their peers say, so this is the ideal time to ensure that children have plenty of opportunities for group discussions. Circle time each day is an excellent way to prioritise this, and it also helps children to get to know everyone in the group rather than just their special friends.

You can use the time to:
- share individuals' news
- talk about the current theme or topic
- discuss what children have done that day
- make plans for the future – this can be in the very short term, for instance planning what children would like to do that day, or longer term such as looking forward to a special event

- model being a considerate and reactive partner in interactions with others – 'Thank you for that cup of tea, Harry. It was lovely. Do you know, I think I'm feeling a bit hungry now ...'
- encourage children to ask others questions about what they say
- play games that involve listening and responding to one another – see the 'Sound circle' activity on page 58.

Specific areas

Literacy

According to the EYFS framework, literacy development involves encouraging children to link sounds and letters and to begin to read and write. Children must be given access to a wide range of reading materials (books, poems, and other written materials) to ignite their interest.

The roots of literacy

Two of the prime areas of learning and development – communication and language and physical development – and the 'playing and exploring' characteristic of effective learning provide the foundations for literacy. Literacy and communication and language are linked inseparably – children cannot progress with reading and writing unless they are progressing in terms of their understanding and use of communication and language. Physical development provides the foundations for handwriting, with an ELG relating to handwriting and other mark making.

Opportunities to engage in literacy activities should be provided in all areas of early years settings, both inside and out. In high quality settings, unlimited access to a range of activities to support literacy development, such as mark making, is made available. Your role is to support what children are learning and to provide opportunities to extend learning when children are ready.

Emergent writing

When children first attempt to write, they tend to draw rows of patterns and shapes that look similar to letters. They will eventually include some letters amongst the patterns and shapes, although they may be muddled – perhaps back to front. This early writing is often referred to as 'emergent' (because writing is an emerging skill in this stage of a child's development). Children benefit from frequent practice at emergent writing, and this can be effectively provided through play.

> **❗ Don't forget**
>
> --
>
> Children may begin to read independently around the age of 7, although there is a wide variation in this. As time progresses, most children will go on to read and write, and understand more complex words and text.

The ELGs

There are two ELGs for this specific area of learning and development:

1. Reading (see below)

2. Writing (see page 138).

Each one is explained in detail in the relevant section that follows.

Reading

> **◉ Early learning goal**
>
> --
>
> **Reading**: Children read and understand simple sentences. They use phonic knowledge to decode regular words and read them aloud accurately. They also read some common irregular words. They demonstrate understanding when talking with others about what they have read.

Ask Miranda!

Q: What do 'phonics' and 'phonic knowledge' mean?

A: The National Literacy Trust has a good definition for 'phonics':

'Phonics refers to a method for teaching speakers of English to read and write the language. Phonics involves connecting the sounds of spoken English with letters or groups of letters (e.g. that the sound /k/ can be represented by c, k, ck or ch spellings) and teaching them to blend the sounds of letters together to produce approximate pronunciations of unknown words. In this way phonics enables people to use individual sounds to construct words. For example, when taught the sounds for the letters *t, p, a* and *s*, one can build up the words 'tap', 'pat', 'pats', 'taps' and 'sat'.

In the early years, children learn the phonetic sounds of letters. The term 'phonetic knowledge' simply refers to the phonic sounds that they already know. By the end of the EYFS, many children will use their phonetic knowledge to both read and write down words.

Activity ideas

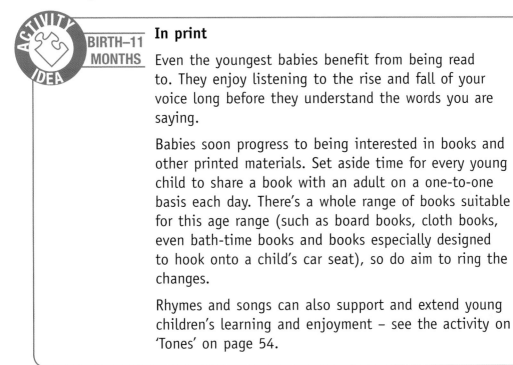

BIRTH–11 MONTHS

In print

Even the youngest babies benefit from being read to. They enjoy listening to the rise and fall of your voice long before they understand the words you are saying.

Babies soon progress to being interested in books and other printed materials. Set aside time for every young child to share a book with an adult on a one-to-one basis each day. There's a whole range of books suitable for this age range (such as board books, cloth books, even bath-time books and books especially designed to hook onto a child's car seat), so do aim to ring the changes.

Rhymes and songs can also support and extend young children's learning and enjoyment – see the activity on 'Tones' on page 54.

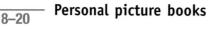

Personal picture books

8–20 MONTHS

During this stage, children increasingly respond when books and printed materials, songs and rhymes are shared with them. So it is a good time to focus on making these activities as personal to individual children as possible.

One effective way of doing this is to create personal picture books for individual children. You can use small photo albums for this or make your own version from card if you prefer – see the 'All about books' activity on page 163 of the 'Understanding the world' section.

You can also use children's names in some songs and rhymes to capture and hold their interest whilst making the experience more meaningful for them. The 'Very nice to see you' song, which is sung as a greeting to each child during circle time at many early years settings, is a good example of this.

❗ Don't forget

The National Literacy Trust has an excellent range of free resources for early years practitioners, including tips on storytelling, recommended book lists and even an audit which will help you identify improvements you could make to your book corner. Visit www.literacytrust.org.uk.

Familiar feel

16–36 MONTHS

Children learn much from repetition and, within this age range, children can thrive on the opportunity to revisit stories, books, songs, rhymes and so on. This can enable children to:
- develop favourites, which helps to ignite the reading spark and foster a love of stories and words
- get to know stories/books/rhymes well enough to

actively join in with the telling or reciting of them (for instance, if you pause they may 'read' the next word or so)
- get to know stories/books/rhymes well enough to enjoy the anticipation of what comes next
- use familiar stories in their own play
- feel engaged with familiar story characters and visual aids, such as puppets and story sacks (see the 'Visual aids' activity and the Development matters! feature on story sacks on page 57).

The benefit for a child is extended when both the early years setting and their parents and carers are aware of the stories, books, songs etc. that the child is currently experiencing. (Remember that some children may only attend the setting once a week.) Try the following activities to increase parents' and carers' awareness:
- Create a wall display around stories – you could feature the main characters of a book, for instance.
- Create story sacks for families to borrow.
- Invite parents to spend some time with their children in your book corner.
- Encourage children to show parents books they are interested in.
- Send home the words of songs and rhymes children are learning.
- Make recordings of the group sharing songs and rhymes, and share them with families (for instance, you could send out audio or video clips by email).

Figure 3.13 Rereading favourite stories helps develop a love of stories and words

A unique child: observing what children are learning

Excerpt from a free description observation of a 3-year-old child which documents how the love of a favourite story motivates him to share a book with his friend:

> Harry enters the book corner with his friend Rochelle. He starts looking through the books. He says, 'Where is the trains?' Rochelle takes a book from the shelf, sits on a beanbag and turns the pages. Harry says, 'Where is the trains?' He pushes books onto the floor as he looks through them.

> An adult approaches and says, 'What are you doing, Harry?' Harry says, 'Looking for the trains.' The adult replies, 'The book about the trains is on the big chair because we're having it at story time today. You can get it if you like ... or you could look at another book now and save the train story for later.'

> Harry goes to the big chair, picks up the book and takes it to the book corner. He sits next to Rochelle. He shows her the cover of the book saying, 'The train one.'

30–50 MONTHS

Make it meaningful

At this stage, children will be learning that print carries meaning. It's helpful for practitioners to support this by creating plenty of opportunities for children to see adults reading and writing for real purposes. So why not build these opportunities into everyday routines?

For example, you could try the following:

- Begin snack time by asking everyone what they would like to drink, and write this down on a list. This can be given to the practitioner who will fetch the drinks. When the practitioner returns with the drinks, they can read out the list of who is having what to make sure that everyone gets what they wanted and demonstrate the purpose of the list to the children.

- In a group setting with more than one room, children and staff can send notes (containing news about something or someone within the setting) to one another. For example, a note about Kelly's new sibling or an invitation to another activity going on in the setting, such as a music session. This can create a lot of excitement!

- Make your own charts incorporating meaningful print and refer to them each day, for instance you may have a daily job rota on which children can look for their name. They will be keen to find out whose turn it is to help with tasks, such as feeding the nursery pet or watering the plants.

Development matters!

Positive relationships: what adults could do

When Anita shares books on a one-to-one basis with the children at her setting, she runs her finger along the sentences as she reads, to show that she is following the text. Often she sees the children copying this technique when they are 'playing reading' to a doll or teddy. This shows that the children are learning that, when a story is being read, the words being said relate to words on the page.

❶ Don't forget

Regular bilingual story sessions can be achieved by:

- inviting parents or librarians speaking another language to visit at story time and to translate a story as it unfolds
- borrowing bilingual story books from the local children's library – these provide the text in both English and an additional language, and are an excellent resource for introducing children to print in languages other than English.

Development matters!

Positive relationships: what adults could do

When it comes to recognising words, children usually recognise their own name first. You can help by providing children with plenty of opportunities to see and look for their name. For example, you could:

- display children's names above the coat pegs and ask them to find their peg
- put pieces of card with their names on the table where they have lunch and invite them to find their seat.

You can also provide labels on familiar objects (such as on your boxes of resources) or in familiar places (such as the book corner).

Help children to learn both the names of letters and the sounds that they make. Children often learn the sounds of letters within their own name first.

Development matters!

Positive relationships: what adults could do

Melita has recently started a new job as a supervisor at a pre-school. She has noticed that children do not seem to spend long looking at books in the book corner, and that adults do not frequently join the children there. Melita feels that the book corner could be more inviting and attractive.

Melita raises the issue at a staff meeting. On reflection, the team feel that they may have been neglecting this part of the environment. It seems that the same books have been in the book corner for a long time, and that some of them are in a tatty condition. Nothing new has been done in terms of the way the area is presented for several months. Melita has also noted that the book corner is sited between the messy area and the sinks, which means there is a busy footfall of children passing.

Melita and the team agree that the book corner needs reinvigorating. They decide to move the whole area to a quieter position that enjoys good natural light from the window. At the same time they will do a stock take of the books, and remove any that are in poor condition. Melita allocates a small budget for replenishing the stock, and the staff also agree on a rota that will ensure that they take turns to regularly supplement and refresh the books by borrowing from the local children's library. Melita asks each member of staff to ensure that they spend some time sharing books with children in the book corner each day, and to think about varying ways in which the book corner can be set up in a stimulating, attractive fashion.

Melita intends to monitor the impact of the changes. She also plans to observe and reflect on group story times as soon as possible.

❶ Don't forget

In early years settings there should be a broad range of high quality resources to support children's learning in both reading and writing. They should be presented in ways that are accessible, attractive and stimulating – see the 'It's a small world' activity on page 64. Ringing the changes regularly and monitoring the use of resources is crucial to achieving this. If resources are not inspiring creative and imaginative play of different types, it's a good idea for practitioners to work together to refresh current practice. It may be that investment in different resources is required, along with the introduction of some new activities.

Library visit

40–60 MONTHS

It's good practice to encourage children in this age band to add to their first-hand experience of the world through the use of books, other texts and information, and ICT (information and communication technology).

A visit to a children's library in a small group is an excellent way to promote this. It's important to remember that, while some children will be library members and be taken regularly to choose books by their families, others may never visit a library with a parent throughout their childhood. You can record the library visit using pictures and words to create a book about the visit.

You will need:
- A camera
- A printer
- A scrapbook
- A pen
- A glue stick
- Library membership for your setting

What to do:

1. When planning, give some thought to the focus of the visit. It's a good idea to vary this. For example, children may be tasked with changing the setting's library books, perhaps by choosing two or three story books each. Or, you may want children to search for

books on a particular theme, such as the post office and writing letters, or starting school, or pets. These books can span both fiction and non-fiction.

2. Now think about how you are going to promote the concept of 'finding information' in a library. You may want children to find some specific information by looking something up in a reference book or other texts. For example, if the current theme is autumn, perhaps they could look up the name of the tree that produces the conkers they've seen on the setting's interest table.

3. Think too about the ICT facilities – most libraries stock story book and CD sets, and loan out DVDs and CD-ROMs. Many have access to computers. Children may also be introduced to microfiche (archived material stored on microfilm, including newspaper articles and photographs), which is viewed via a special screen with a viewer.

4. Finally, contact the library or check online to find out if there are regular story time sessions, and whether storytellers also visit. You may like to plan your visit to coincide with these. Also, check if the library will be happy for you to take photos of your visit on their premises.

5. On the day of the outing, talk with children about the purpose of their library visit, and explain how you will be making a book all about it.

6. Take photos of each aspect of the visit – the journey there, the tasks undertaken at the library and the journey back. Be sure to include a photographic record of key aspects, such as checking out new books.

7. Print the photos. Discuss with the children what is happening in each one, and help them to stick the photos into a scrapbook in the right sequence. Collaborate with the children to create and write in captions for each of the photos.

8. Share the book with the whole group at circle time or story time.

Figure 3.14 There may be regular story time sessions at the library

Writing

⊙ *Early learning goal*

Writing: Children use their phonic knowledge to write words in ways that match their spoken sounds. They also write some irregular common words. They write simple sentences which can be read by themselves and others. Some words are spelled correctly and others are phonetically plausible.

The Development Matters guidance states that children's later writing is based on skills and understandings which they develop as babies and toddlers. Before they can write, they need to learn to use spoken language to communicate. Later they learn to write down the words they can say. Early mark making is not the same as writing. It is a sensory and physical experience for babies and toddlers, which they do not yet connect to forming symbols which can communicate meaning.

Activity ideas

As it is important that children develop their spoken language before their written language, activities are not included in this section for birth to 26 months. For this age range, you can instead refer to the activities in the 'Communication and language' section (pages 54–72) which develop the communication skills that are the roots of writing, and the activities in the 'Physical development' section related to mark making and writing. (The roots of mark making and handwriting are developed further through the 'Playing and exploring' characteristic of effective learning.)

22–36 MONTHS

Signs and symbols

At this age, children are learning that signs and signals carry meaning. You can help them to understand this by regularly drawing children's attention to the signs and symbols around them in their everyday environments, both in the setting and when out on visits, and by talking about their meanings.

For example, you can help children to recognise that the pounds and pence symbols they see in shops (both real shops and in imaginary shop areas) refer to money. You can draw their attention to the male and female symbols used on toilet doors. In group settings there will be exit signs above every outside door. Once children are familiar with these, you can encourage them to spot the signs in other public locations, and to identify what they are communicating.

You can also use symbols/pictures on boxes of stored resources to tell children what they'll find inside (such as a drawing of a Lego brick), and use symbols above coat pegs (such as the outline of a car or a boat). Children can be tasked with identifying their own coat peg each morning by looking for the symbol they are given that day.

You may also like to create a simple register to use with children at circle time. A tick can indicate a child is present and a circle can indicate that they are absent.

❗ Don't forget

It's good practice for children to have an environment that is 'rich in print'. But do make sure that any printed material (such as signs and symbols) makes sense to children, and that it is refreshed regularly. After a while we tend to stop noticing things we see every day.

Development matters!

Enabling environments: what adults could provide

It's important for practitioners to provide plentiful, wide-ranging opportunities for writing/mark making all over the setting, both inside and out.

There are some excellent ways to do this via role play, for example, you could turn an area into:

- an imaginary restaurant – provide notepads and pens for the children to take orders
- an imaginary doctors' surgery – provide individual paper chains for the children to make name bracelets
- an imaginary shop – provide stickers for the children to write out prices and 'special offer' signs and symbols.

But remember to provide wider opportunities (mark-making materials, listening equipment etc.) in the construction area or book corner.

Post office

30–50 MONTHS

At this stage, it's good practice to model writing for a purpose and to provide children with activities that experiment with writing. This activity provides an opportunity to use writing within the context of a role play based in a post office. It also enables you to recycle unwanted junk mail!

You will need:

- A collection of junk mail, including forms to 'fill in' and pre-addressed envelopes
- Additional envelopes – these can include new ones alongside used ones which have been opened carefully and are still intact. Aim to include a range of sizes, colours and types (manila, padded etc.)
- Different types of letter writing paper, such as note pads, plain white A4 sheets, individual coloured A5 sheets
- Used stamps saved from envelopes
- New stamps – this needn't be expensive as you can purchase a number of 1p stamps for role-play purposes (a bargain at £1 for 100!)
- Books about a post office, postal workers and/or characters writing and sending letters or parcels, such as *Postman Pat*
- Pencils and pens
- Glue sticks
- A table-top area to serve as a counter
- A play till and money
- An ink pad and stamp set
- A post box

What to do:

1. Involve parents and colleagues in collecting junk mail and saving used stamps and envelopes for a period before the activity – three weeks is usually ideal for a group setting. Remind them to ensure that any confidential or inappropriate material is not collected up. (This tends to be a popular activity and you could be surprised by how much mail you get through!)

2. If possible, take children on a visit to the local post office, and arrange for them to have a tour of the 'back of shop' area to see what happens and how things are done. If this isn't possible, you may decide instead to invite a post office worker to visit the setting. (See the community visitor activity on page 166 of the 'Understanding the world' section.) Take particular note of the forms available which people fill in and return for a number of reasons (such as car tax forms to allow them to drive their car on the roads, as well as the stamps people buy and the letters and parcels they post).

3. To set the scene, you can also read stories and non-fiction books (for example, the *Postman Pat* series, the *Jolly Postman* series and

Postman Pete) that feature a post office, postal workers and/or characters writing and sending letters or parcels.

4. You're now ready for the activity! Set out a post office counter area featuring the till and money, pencils/pens, stamps to sell, ink pads and a stamp set. Set up a behind-the-counter area for storing posted parcels etc. and ensure there is a prominent post box. (Many settings have a post box which they use periodically for role play and for times such as Christmas when children post cards to one another. But it is also easy to make one with the children from a rectangular cardboard box of the appropriate size. Cut out a slot, paint it red and it will be instantly recognisable.)

5. Close by, set out a table containing all of the writing materials, used stamps, envelopes, forms (you have collected whilst at the post office or any other pro formas, such as those that you may have got from junk mail) and glue sticks. At first it's a good idea to model how to fill in a form or write a letter – 'I need to fill in this form and take it to the post office to be able to drive my car', or 'I'm going to write a letter to my Gran. Then I'll stick a stamp on and post it in the post box'.

6. You're likely to see lots of emergent writing from the children, and they are often inspired to copy some words and letters that they see printed on the junk mail and used envelopes.

Extension ideas: There are a number of extension possibilities. Children could go on to role play delivering the mail, for instance (see the activity on the 'post office' on page 150 in the 'Mathematics' section), or they could actually send a picture and accompanying letter to their home, addressed to themselves or a family member. You could also involve families by asking them to send a letter to the setting with their child. The child can then have the pleasure of opening it.

◆ *Development matters!*

Positive relationships: what adults could do

Juanita has been promoting writing by allowing children to see her writing for real purposes. She decides to extend this by introducing a new 'daily diary' activity into the setting's routine. At the end of the

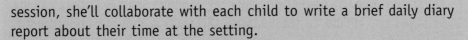

session, she'll collaborate with each child to write a brief daily diary report about their time at the setting.

To do this, Juanita talks with each child on a one-to-one basis about what they have done that day, and any significant events, such as an activity they particularly enjoyed. She lets them see her writing down what they have told her. Later, each child enjoys sharing the information with their parents or carers at home.

Juanita's activity underpins the fact that print can carry personal meaning for each of us.

❗ Don't forget

Give children opportunities to see words and letters so that they can try to copy them when they are making marks. For instance, you may place children's name cards on the drawing table and invite them to find their seat. They may then attempt to copy their names since all the materials will be at hand.

40–60+
MONTHS

Word banks

A word bank is a storage place for a collection of written words that children have learned. Each word is written on a separate card. Children can go to the word bank to explore words, or when they want to copy a word or check a spelling. The word cards can be stored in a number of ways – in folders, on magnetic boards, on wall displays or hung on a washing line by pegs.

Children in this age group will be in the early stages of beginning to use word banks. Word banks are generally used on an ongoing basis with children throughout their primary school years, and in time will focus on increasingly complex sets of words, such as nouns, verbs and adjectives. There will be an expectation that children use the words in their conversations and writing. But when first using word banks with young children, it is helpful to decide on a clear topic for each collection, such as 'summer words'. Topics can be linked to theme work the setting may be undertaking.

To create a word bank, start by introducing the topic to children and spend some time talking around it. Make use of open questions – 'What sort of places do we visit in the summer?' 'What do we do there?' 'What do we take with us?' 'What is the weather like?' 'What do we wear?' Let the children see you writing down the words they suggest.

Once the bank has been created, remember to use it! For instance, you may ask children to take turns to choose a word and bring it back to the group at circle time – this can be the starting point for a discussion. For example, if a child brings back the word 'lollipop' from a summer word bank, it may provoke conversation about flavours, ice-cream vans and cooling down on a hot day. This task helps to consolidate that print carries meaning and, as children look at the cards, you can also sound out phonetically the segments of simple words.

❗ Don't forget

When children are able to write their name and some letters, they can begin copying simple words. Many children learn to do this by writing simple captions for their artwork: 'a dog', 'my doll' etc.

⬡ Development matters!

A unique child: observing what children are learning

Excerpt from a free description observation of a 5-year-old which demonstrates how a word bank is helping children at one setting to write their first words.

Ellis puts down his crayon and says, 'Finished'. He picks up his paper and takes it to his key worker, Sandi. He shows her the picture and says, 'It's Georgie.' Sandi replies, 'Oh yes. Your Georgie is a friendly cat, isn't she? She likes you to stroke her lovely fur ... are you going to write anything on your paper?' Ellis nods and goes to the animal-themed word bank (displayed on a magnetic board). He selects the word 'cat' and takes it back to the drawing table. He selects a pencil and, referring to the card, copies the word 'cat' beneath his drawing. He then slowly and carefully writes his name in the top left-hand corner ...

Mathematics

According to the EYFS framework, mathematics involves providing children with opportunities to develop and improve their skills in counting, understanding and using numbers, calculating simple addition and subtraction problems; and to describe shapes, spaces, and measures.

The word 'mathematics' can conjure up an image of quite formal teaching and learning, so it's important for practitioners to remember that early years activities should promote play and exploration. Over the next few pages, you will see that in every setting there are many diverse, naturally occurring opportunities to promote aspects of children's mathematical development. For example, tidying up involves the mathematical skill of sorting; fetching the right number of plates at snack time involves counting; and sharing out slices of apple involves division. Opportunities to engage in playful planned activities that promote mathematics can easily be provided in all areas of the setting, both inside and out.

The ELGs

There are two ELGs for this specific area of learning and development:

1. Numbers (see page 146)

2. Shape, space and measures (see page 153).

Each one is explained in detail in the relevant section that follows.

Numbers

> ### ⊙ Early learning goal
>
> **Numbers:** Children count reliably with numbers from 1 to 20, place them in order and say which number is one more or one less than a given number. Using quantities and objects, they add and subtract two single-digit numbers and count on or back to find the answer. They solve problems, including doubling, halving and sharing.

Activity ideas

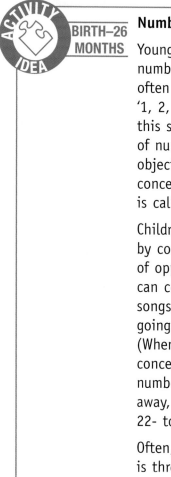

BIRTH–26 MONTHS

Number and counting rhymes

Young children will count by rote (they will recite numbers as they would a nursery rhyme, and indeed often learn to do this from nursery rhymes such as '1, 2, 3, 4, 5, Once I caught a fish alive') but, at this stage, they don't really understand the meaning of numbers or counting. Encourage children to touch objects as they count to help them to understand the concept of counting and numbers – this understanding is called 'one-to-one correspondence'.

Children will muddle or miss out numbers at first – help by counting along with them and giving them plenty of opportunities to count, for instance together you can count out the cups at snack time, or use counting songs and rhymes, or count the steps to the slide when going up them – the everyday possibilities are endless. (When children have a secure understanding of the concept of number, they can begin to understand simple number operations, such as adding one or taking one away, although this is not expected until around the 22- to 36-month age band.)

Often, the first introduction children have to number is through number rhymes and counting songs. Learn and use as many of these as you can, including those from other cultures and in other languages. Help babies and young children to recognise the rhythm patterns by clapping their hands to the rhythms or swaying with them. Through these activities even the youngest babies will begin to become familiar with number names, and will enjoy them.

Development matters!

A unique child: observing what children are learning

Excerpt from a checklist observation of a 24-month-old child showing early mathematical development.

Activity	Yes	No	Date	Observer's comments
Looks for things which are currently out of sight, e.g. favourite toy	✔		29/9/12	
Uses some counting words in play (unlikely to be in context)	✔		29/9/12	Often 'counts' objects when resources are unpacked, saying numbers he knows randomly
Is beginning to sort a few items into basic sets	✔		29/9/12	Enjoys helping to tidy up resources. Carries out instructions such as, 'Please put this away with the other dolls'. Responds to, for example, 'Which box do these cars belong in?' Will divide mixed items into two sets, e.g. socks and toys.
Joins in with counting and number rhymes	✔		29/9/12	With enjoyment. Will copy adult's actions, holding up fingers for counting etc.

Sorting and matching laundry

22–36 MONTHS

Why not try a sorting role play with children towards the end of this age range? It's a fun challenge and involves using mathematics for an everyday purpose. You may like to change your appearance in some way to show that you are in character if you work in a group setting – perhaps by wearing an apron that covers the uniform you wear for work.

What you will need:
- A laundry basket
- A selection of laundry including:
  - several pairs of socks in different colours, sizes and patterns
  - a few odd socks
  - other similar types of item to sort together, such as six children's T-shirts, four skirts
- An apron

What to do:
1. Enter the home corner carrying the basket full of laundry. Say 'hello' to the children and tell them your character's name. Explain that you have just taken the laundry in from the washing line in your garden.
2. Ask children to help you to sort it into sets so it's ready to put away. The socks will need to be matched into pairs first. Demonstrate putting the items into sets, and be sure to show children how to find pairs of socks that match.
3. At the end of the activity, acknowledge that there are some odd socks left over and that you will have to look for them. Ask for suggestions of where to look. (Answers might include the washing machine, on the washing line, in the linen basket.)
4. Thank children for their efforts and exit, explaining that you are off to put the washing away.

Extension ideas: You may like to:
- Set up a makeshift washing line in the garden and hang out some odd socks for children to find, and/or hide some odd socks in the washing machine in the home corner for children to find.
- Ask children to sort laundry into other types of set, for example, by colour.
- In mixed age groups, ask the older children to sort the winter clothes from the summer clothes.

Development matters!

Enabling environments: what adults could provide

The following resources/equipment can be used to promote number recognition; sorting skills; counting, matching and number operations:

- counting beads
- sorting trays
- diverse objects to sort
- number cards or tiles, magnetic numbers
- number friezes/posters
- a number line
- number signs, notices, symbols and labels
- a cash till
- money.

30–50 MONTHS

Recognising and writing numbers

Children who have a good understanding of the concept of number will find it easier to learn to recognise written numbers because the number symbols that we use will have meaning to them. Children learn to recognise numbers when they see them frequently in their environment and come across them in their play. They can see numbers:

- on wall displays
- on calendars
- on board games
- in imaginary areas (prices on food in the 'shop' perhaps).

As adults refer to these numbers, children begin to remember them.

Children often learn to recognise numbers with personal meaning first – the number on their front door, or their age.

You can help by making number cards and asking children to match the written number with a number of objects (such as the number of toy cars you have set out). Introduce one or two numbers at a time.

Learning the symbols is difficult for children. Encourage children to practise writing numbers informally, for instance provide stickers and pencils in the imaginary shop area and let children price some items themselves, or draw out numbered stepping stones for children to follow outside, providing chalk so they can draw and number their own too.

ACTIVITY IN FOCUS

30-50 MONTHS

Post office

In the 'Literacy' section you were introduced to a post office activity (see page 140). You can extend this to provide an opportunity for a group of children to recognise and match numbers by sending and delivering post to particular house numbers.

What you will need:
- A sheet – for placing over a table or for handing between chairs
- Stickers
- Pens
- Envelopes
- A post box

What to do:
1. Enable each child to create their own home, den or base – this can be done simply by placing a sheet over a table or hanging some fabric across the gap between two chairs.
2. Help children to give their homes a number – they may choose to have the number they see on their own real door at home. Write the number on a sticker and get the children to place it somewhere prominent on their 'home'.

3. When the children role play writing letters, encourage them to put a number on their envelopes before putting them in the post box – they can copy the numbers from the stickers made earlier. Children may send letters to their friends and/or themselves.

4. Enable the children to take turns to play the postman or postwoman. It's their job to empty the post box and, using their number recognition skills, deliver the mail to the houses.

5. Inside their 'homes', children can enjoy opening the letters they receive.

Living board game

40–60+ MONTHS

Children in this age range will be familiar with how basic board games work – they throw a dice and move a counter the corresponding number of places on the board, and the first one to reach the end of the board wins. This activity takes that idea but on a larger scale.

• Start by explaining to children that you are going to play a giant-sized board game outside in the playground. The children themselves are going to be the counters – they will throw a dice and then move around the board.

• Next, involve children in helping you to draw out a playing board on the ground with chalk. You can choose any shape – a snake perhaps, a straight line, a circle or a figure of eight. Divide the shape into playing squares large enough for two or three children to stand on (as they may land on the same square). Children may like to decorate the playing squares with chalk.

• Ideally, you'll play the game using a large dice – a foam variety approximately the size of a football is available and is an excellent option for outside use. You will need to take the dice to each player in turn so they do not lose their place on the board by going to fetch it. Encourage each player to recognise the number they have thrown for themselves, and to count out the corresponding number of spaces as they move forwards on the board.

Extension idea: Instead of asking children to move the number of spaces that correspond to the number they have thrown on the dice, ask them to repeat an action that will move them forwards on the board. The number of repetitions should correspond to the number they have thrown on the dice. For example, a child may jump forward three times, stopping in the space on the board that they land in on the last jump. This enables children to count actions (instead of the more commonplace occupation of counting objects). If children land on a line on the board, allow them to step into the space in front of them. Let them decide how they want to move each time for themselves – hopping, skipping, jumping etc.

Figure 3.15 By the end of the EYFS, most children will reliably count up to ten everyday objects

Development matters!

Positive relationships: what adults could do

Pre-school worker, Nikos, has planned a range of activities with his group of 4- to 5-year-olds to consolidate and extend their mathematical understanding:

- counting how many cups are needed at snack time
- sharing out the slices of apple at snack time
- singing number songs/rhymes and stopping to explore the number operations (for example 'We had five fire engines but one drove away. How many are left now?')
- tidying up – involving sorting objects and positioning (for example 'That goes on the shelf')
- finding the number that corresponds to each child's age on the number line
- counting how many treats are left for the nursery rabbit and writing down the number.

Shape, space and measures

Early learning goal

Shape, space and measures: Children use everyday language to talk about size, weight, capacity, position, distance, time and money to compare quantities and objects and to solve problems. They recognise, create and describe patterns. They explore characteristics of everyday objects and shapes, and use mathematical language to describe them.

Activity ideas

The Development Matters guidance states that babies' early awareness of shape, space and measures grows from their sensory awareness and opportunities to observe objects and their movements, and to play and explore. Specific activities relating to shape, space and measures are not, therefore, included for this age range. Further information about the early awareness of shape, space and measures is included in the 'Physical development' section and is developed further through the 'Playing and exploring' characteristic of effective learning.

ACTIVITY IDEA

8–20 MONTHS

Differences in scale and shape

In this age band, children are beginning to recognise big and small in meaningful contexts – for instance, that a toy car is small and a real car is big, that their coat is small and their key worker's coat is big.

They are also getting to know what objects are like and how they can change, for instance how malleable objects can be squashed up small or stretched out long. They're also learning how they can change the shape of their own bodies intentionally (curling up small and stretching up high, for example) and enjoy activities that involve exploring this.

You can support this by:
- singing songs like 'Jingle jangle scarecrow' and doing the actions together (this entails bobbing down on the ground and then popping up)
- enabling children in this age band to join with older children for music and movement sessions in which they explore actions, such as curling up like an acorn and slowly growing and stretching into a tree
- sorting objects according to size, for instance having two boxes out at tidy-up time, one for small balls and one for large balls
- sharing books showing objects of different sizes and using story props (such as three bowls of different sizes when telling the tale of 'Goldilocks and the three bears') to support children.

Guide to the learning and development requirements

16–26 MONTHS

Shaping up

Children in this age band will be learning to recognise shapes and to know their names. They usually learn the basic shapes first – circle, square, rectangle and triangle. You can help children by:

- encouraging them to recognise shapes when they come across them ('What shape is the window in the picture?')
- referring to different shapes and patterns in the everyday environment and daily activities ('Let's sit at the square table')
- using shape sorters, shape board games and basic jigsaw puzzles (which encourage shape and spatial awareness).

Shapes are often one of the first sets children are able to sort by.

Why not involve parents and carers in the learning children do about shapes within the setting? You can explain to them what children are currently learning and how you are supporting them, and encourage them to do the same. Ask parents to look around their homes and help children to spot shapes and patterns in their everyday environments, for instance the washing machine door is a circle.

You can also encourage children to bring in appropriate shapes from home to share with you and their peers, as the Development matters! feature below demonstrates.

Development matters!

Positive relationships: what adults could do

Children's centre worker, Naveen, has been involving parents and carers in the learning children do about shapes within the setting. Today, 2-year-old Scarlet arrives at the setting full of excitement. She's holding a wicker coaster which she has brought from home.

She rushes up to Naveen and shows him, saying 'My circle! Look!'
She then rushes to another adult and holds out the coaster proudly.
Scarlet's mother explains that she, Scarlet and Scarlet's father had
been looking for shapes in their home the evening before. Scarlet was
thrilled with the prospect of bringing in the coaster to show everyone
when her mother suggested it. She had even eaten her breakfast
while clinging onto it that morning.

Naveen is pleased that Scarlet has been so excited and proud about
recognising shapes. As soon as she has waved Scarlet's mother
goodbye, Naveen takes Scarlet on a visit to the room next door so
she can share her circle with another two adults.

ACTIVITY IDEA | 22–36 MONTHS

Volume and capacity

Volume and capacity are difficult concepts to
understand. Young children, however, can make informal
discoveries about them which will be the foundations
of their understanding. You can assist this process
by providing vessels of different sizes for children to
play with in the sand and water trays. They may then
discover that a bucket holds three beakers full of water,
for instance. You can also help children to learn about
volume and capacity when tidying up, such as the large
box will hold all the wooden blocks but they will not all
fit into the small box.

You can play alongside children and draw their
attention to these concepts. For instance, you may say,
'I wonder if I can pour all the water in this bottle into
my yoghurt pot ... no, look, I can't. The yoghurt pot is
full and there's still water left in the bottle. I wonder if
a bottle full of water will fill up two yoghurt pots ...'

Figure 3.16 Playing with different sized containers in the sand tray helps children understand about volume and capacity

The following resources/equipment can be used to support weighing, measuring and exploring shape, space, and the concept of time:

- scales
- weights
- rulers
- measures
- height charts
- shape sorters
- shape puzzles
- differently shaped construction resources
- clocks
- watches
- time lines.

Excerpt from a free description observation of a 26-month-old child which demonstrates her ability to sort items by type and shape.

> Siobhan (S) is playing with the cars on the carpet. A practitioner (P) says it's time to tidy up. S goes to the shelf and looks at the boxes. P says, 'What do you want to put away?' S points to the cars. P says, 'Can you see the right box? With the picture of a car on?' S points to the right box. P smiles and nods. S picks it up and takes it back to the cars. She starts to put them in. Another child who is also tidying approaches, drops several board books into the box and walks away. S looks into the box. She pauses for several seconds. She then starts to take the books out, tossing them onto the carpet. When this is done, she resumes putting the cars into the box ...

❶ Don't forget

Children generally draw shapes and patterns before they learn to write numbers. Children need opportunities to observe both patterns in nature and artificial patterns, along with resources that enable them to copy or extend the patterns which interest them. You can also explore the patterns found within various cultures, such as Rangoli (Indian folk art) patterns.

Development matters!

Enabling environments: what adults could provide

Most children do not fully understand the abstract concept of time until they are in at least their seventh year. Younger children, however, can be encouraged to recognise the concept of time through the provision of a routine, for instance after snack time it is story time.

Children can be encouraged to understand what is meant by 'today', 'yesterday' and 'tomorrow' by talking about past events and planning.

The more distant past can also be referred to. Most 4-year-olds will recall their last birthday, for instance, or a festival significant to their family, such as Christmas or Hanukah. Ensure the environment features wall displays, calendars and plans which incorporate photos to promote this. You can also make personal photo-books, or collect mementos to keep in memory boxes, and record video and audio clips to share at a later date.

30–50 MONTHS

The measure of things

Measuring refers to the measurement of weight, length, volume and capacity. Before children can effectively learn about the formal measurement of these using numbers, they need to learn about the concept of measurement.

Use simple balancing scales to help children to understand the concepts of weight measurement – heavier, lighter; heaviest, lightest. Allow children to feel the weights themselves to reinforce the concept and to help children learn to predict weight. Measuring for real purposes is always beneficial, such as measuring out the ingredients when cooking or making play dough. (Do set up a well-resourced cooking station within the environment, if possible.)

Also, introduce the concept of measuring length and distance (long, short; longest, shortest) in simple ways. For example, see how far a group of children can jump and record this with a chalk line. The children can then compare the distances. Or, using string, get them to measure the height of a plant as it grows – they can display each length of string to show the growth over a period of weeks, and take pictures to record the growth.

Positional language

30–50 MONTHS

You can help children to learn positional language – such as 'on', 'under', 'inside', 'on top', 'in front' and 'behind' – through simple games. For example, you could play a game of 'Simon says' which requires children to position themselves in certain ways: 'Simon says sit under a table' or 'Simon says stand on top of the climbing cube' etc.

You could also, with a small group, play a treasure hunt game which relies on positional clues – you might hide something fun for the children to play with, such as pots of bubbles. You can give positional clues as children hunt, such as 'Thomas was getting warm when he looked *inside* the cupboard' or 'Jessie got colder when she looked *behind* the book shelf'.

Extension idea: You may like to create a word bank of simple positional words – see the 'Word banks' activity in the 'Literacy' section on page 143.

2D and 3D shapes

40–60+ MONTHS

At this age, children are generally ready to start using the correct mathematical language for flat 2D shapes and 'solid' 3D shapes, such as a flat round 2D shape is a circle, while a solid round 3D shape is a sphere. You can support this by playing a guessing game with a feely bag.

You will need:
- Items of different 2D and 3D shapes, such as a flat, round coaster and a solid, round tennis ball
- A drawstring bag

What to do:
1. Place one of the objects inside the drawstring bag.
2. Without looking, get one of the children to put their hand inside the bag and describe the shape and feel of the item, using correct mathematical language.

3. You can also ask children funny questions about the item, such as: 'Is it as heavy as an elephant?' 'Is it bigger than a house?' 'Can you go swimming in it?'

4. Finally, ask the child to guess what the object is.

Understanding the world

According to the EYFS framework, understanding the world involves guiding children to make sense of their physical world and their community through opportunities to explore, observe and find out about people, places, technology and the environment.

Ask Miranda!

Q: What is meant by the terms 'physical world' and 'community'?

A: A child's 'physical world' is the environments they are in on any day-to-day basis (the home, the early years setting, the local park, relatives' homes etc.) and other places that they visit less regularly (the beach, a nearby city etc.). It extends to everything that exists in these places, including the landscape, living things, and natural and artificial objects.

A child's 'community' is their local area and the people who live and work within it.

The ELGs

There are three ELGs for this specific area of learning and development:

1. People and communities (see page 162)

2. The world (see page 172)

3. Technology (see page 178).

People and communities

⊙ Early learning goal

People and communities: Children talk about past and present events in their own lives and in the lives of family members. They know that other children don't always enjoy the same things, and are sensitive to this. They know about similarities and differences between themselves and others, and among families, communities and traditions.

Clearly, there are particularly strong links to the prime area of 'Personal, social and emotional development' (see pages 101–127).

Activity ideas

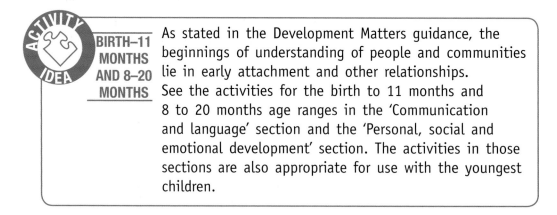

BIRTH–11 MONTHS AND 8–20 MONTHS

As stated in the Development Matters guidance, the beginnings of understanding of people and communities lie in early attachment and other relationships. See the activities for the birth to 11 months and 8 to 20 months age ranges in the 'Communication and language' section and the 'Personal, social and emotional development' section. The activities in those sections are also appropriate for use with the youngest children.

⬡ Development matters!

A unique child: observing what children are learning

Genevieve works in a nursery baby room. She's observing one of her key children, 5-month-old Lewis, as he interacts with her colleague, Becca.

Lewis is making playful babbling sounds, which Becca repeats back to him. After a short time, this develops into a 'conversation'. Becca talks to Lewis, then pauses to allow him to 'reply', then she 'answers' him once again. Becca responds with delight in her facial expressions,

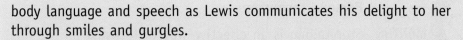

body language and speech as Lewis communicates his delight to her through smiles and gurgles.

Later, when analysing her observation, Genevieve notes that Lewis is forming wider relationships within the setting, and that he shows signs of developing an early awareness of how interactions with others work.

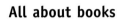

16–26 MONTHS

All about books

To help children to develop awareness of the similarities and differences between themselves and others, and the similarities and differences among families, you can make an 'All about' book for each child. The book will feature both photos and text. There a several ways to make books, but one of the most simple and effective methods for young children is to print out photos and paste them onto stiff pieces of card. Text can then be written directly on the pages by hand, and the pages bound together.

- Ask a child's family for a photo of each person who lives in their home and a photo of the family celebrating a special event together, such as the child's birthday.
- Also take some photos of the child enjoying various activities at your setting, and involve the child's family in choosing which to include in the book.
- Children should choose a photo of themselves for the front cover. It's a good idea to use the child's name in the title of the book, for example 'All about Kai'. You should then write captions for each photo, such as 'This is Kai's big sister. Her name is Macy', or 'Kai loves to play on the slide!' Talk to the child about the captions as you write them.
- It's enjoyable for a child to experience having their own book shared with other children in the group, and to have access to the books of their peers. A child's own 'All about' book is also perfect for a key worker to share with them on a one-to-one basis. Most children like to visit their book regularly.

22–36 MONTHS

Persona resources

Storytelling is an effective way of focusing on the different emotions people have with young children. Props such as puppets, dolls and pictures of people are extremely useful, as children may be able to recognise feelings that they can't yet describe. 'Persona' dolls, puppets or cards are specially designed to show various emotions. For example, in a set of persona puppets there will be faces that look happy, tired, angry, scared etc. You can use persona resources as an aid when reading children a simple story from a book, or you can make up your own simple tale, as in the following Development matters! example below.

Development matters!

A unique child: observing what children are learning

Practitioner Corinne settles a small group of children aged 2½ to 3 years of age on the carpet. She shows them a smiling persona puppet of a boy. She calls him Sam. She asks the children if Sam looks happy – they agree that he does. Corinne replies, 'He does look happy, doesn't he, because he's smiling'. She then shows them another puppet – this time Sam looks sad, and they discuss this briefly. She repeats this with two other puppets, one depicting tiredness and one depicting anger.

Corinne then lays the puppets out in front of her and starts to tell the children a made-up story. She pauses every so often to ask the children to choose a puppet that shows how Sam is feeling at that point. For example, she says, 'It was a lovely day, and Sam's mum had taken him to the park to ride on his tractor. It had big black wheels, just like the one in our garden. Sam put his favourite teddy in front of him on the seat and gave him a ride all around ... I wonder how Sam was feeling then? Can you show me on a puppet? That's right, he was happy, because he was enjoying himself ... But when Sam got home he suddenly realised that he didn't have his teddy. He couldn't find him anywhere. His mum said they must have left him all on his own in the park. Poor teddy! I wonder how Sam was feeling then? Do you think he was still happy ...?' (The story continues – Sam goes back to find his teddy, and is happy to be reunited. But he's very tired after visiting the park twice in one day.)

Figure 3.17 Puppets are useful in helping children to recognise feelings they can't describe

◆ *Development matters!*

Positive relationships: what adults could do

- Pre-school worker Katie is supervising a group of children in the garden. She hears one of the children shrieking excitedly, and turns to see 4-year-old Todd holding his friend Shania's hand tightly, and pulling her along as he runs as fast as he can. Shania, who is 3, is struggling to break free and looks quite frightened.

- Katie steps in, checks that Shania is okay, and then sits down with the children for a chat. They talk about the fact that while Todd enjoys holding hands and running very fast, Shania would much rather run on her own, and prefers to go at her own pace. Todd says, 'But we were having fun'. He seems bewildered by the fact that his friend did not enjoy it too. Katie explains that there are differences and similarities among people – we don't all like and dislike the same things. Todd is anxious to go and play with Shania again. Katie leaves the discussion there for now and suggests that the children play on the climbing frame together, something they both enjoy. But she makes a mental note to explore this area with Todd again.

- When she's next planning activities, Katie decides to create a wall display with the children about their individual likes and dislikes. This can become a focal point for lots of discussion about similarities and differences, and it will be an opportunity to show how important it is to respect these. She decides to consult her colleagues, but she thinks it would be a good idea to include photos of the children doing their favourite activities and with their favourite possessions. She's also thinking about a food-themed display.

Community visitor

30–50 MONTHS

This activity demonstrates how you can make the most of inviting a specific person from your local community to pay a visit to your setting. This creates an opportunity to encourage children to develop positive relationships with community members. It also enables them to explore community roles and, through them, begin to understand community values.

Within your community there will no doubt be a broad range of people you can invite in over time. For example, you might invite in people who have a duty to help us – perhaps a member of one of the emergency services or medical practitioners, such as a doctor, nurse or dentist. Or you might consider people who provide other key local services, such as a farmer, librarian or shopkeeper. You may choose to invite local community members who will go on to become key figures in the children's lives – a reception class teacher, an out of school club playworker or the local crossing guard (lollipop person).

Guide to the learning and development requirements

When choosing who to invite, you might like to consider the wider learning opportunities – for example, inviting a teacher can help prepare children for their transition to school, or inviting a farmer can help children to learn about growing and where food comes from.

What to do:

1. Decide on the type of visitor you'd like (for instance, a police officer) and gain permission to go ahead and organise a visit from the appropriate senior person at your setting. You must comply with any relevant policies/procedures that your setting has in place. It is important to ensure that the visitor is not left unsupervised with children.

2. You may already have a particular person in mind to invite. If not, ask your colleagues for help in tracking down someone who will be suitable. Otherwise, one of the parents/carers may have a relevant connection (or may even be suitable themselves). Failing this, you could just 'cold call' somewhere, such as the local police station, explain what you'd like to do and ask if there's a particular person who you should speak to.

3. Before you actually invite a visitor, think about what it is you would like them to do if they agree to visit – it's the first thing they'll ask you! Why not plan for the visitor and the children to talk about a particular subject (see point 4 below), and then to do something practical with them (see point 5 on the next page).

4. It's a good idea to talk to children about the visitor in advance, and to introduce them to the subject the visitor will talk to them about (such as their job role). Then you and the children can come up with a list of questions to ask during the visit. This helps the children to get the most out of the event, and to engage and interact with the visitor. You can refer to the list during the visit and use your notes to prompt the children, for example 'Felix, you wanted to ask a question about police dogs didn't you?' This strategy can also help the visitor. Some visitors (such as a children's librarian) will be used to talking to groups of children regularly, and will be at ease with them. Other visitors (such as a shopkeeper) who may not have done this before could find the prospect of 'giving a talk' daunting – they may feel much more at ease about coming along to answer some questions.

▶

5.   Planning something practical the visitor and children can do together will extend children's learning and provide further opportunities for engagement and interaction with the visitor. For example, if a shopkeeper is visiting, you could turn the imaginary area into a shop, stocked with real items for children to buy and sell. The shopkeeper could bring along a pricing gun with them. They can demonstrate how it works, then help children to use it to price the goods in their shop. Or, a librarian could read a story to children, then help them to retell it using puppets. A farmer might bring in a tomato plant which children could plant outside in a grow bag.

6.   At the end of the visit, make sure everyone thanks the visitor. It's also nice to get the children to make a thankyou card to send them. Do try to have a chat with the visitor to evaluate how they thought it went. This will help you to make any improvements to your process in the future. If you feel the visit went well, you may want to ask the visitor if they would be willing to come again.

Development matters!

Enabling environments: what adults could provide

Within the setting, practitioners should promote positive images of all people, reflecting the wider society. That is, they should seek to show, through the way they portray people, that all different kinds of people are valued positively in the setting. This can be done by ensuring that the pictures children and young people see in books and displays, on puzzles etc. show males and females; people of all sizes, ethnicities and cultures; and people who have impairments. Positive images should also be reflected in the toys that you choose whenever these represent people. For instance, within the setting's collection of baby dolls you may include dolls of different ethnicities, and within your puppets you may have different ages represented. Your dolls' house may feature a ramp and a doll with a wheelchair, or perhaps crutches, or a hearing aid. The purpose is to represent society's diversity overall – it would be unrealistic to attempt to cover every eventuality in each collection of resources. (Also see the Development matters! feature on page 170 of this section.)

Figure 3.18 Positive images should be reflected in the toys that you choose

❗ Don't forget

Be wary of images that are not positive – in a story or picture, people with disabilities are sometimes shown as being dependent on people without disabilities, perhaps by being cared for or pushed in a wheelchair. Similarly, female characters may be shown as secondary in status to male characters.

Practitioners should ensure that all members of our diverse communities are shown in a positive light. Strong images of those people who may be discriminated against are particularly important. Some examples of available resources that show strong images are:

- a set of jigsaw puzzles that each show a family of a different culture eating a meal together

- a poster on the theme of celebrations, that shows six families of different religions celebrating

- a set of picture postcards showing athletes competing in the Paralympics

- a set of dolls' house dolls, featuring four elderly couples of different ethnicities

- a set of puppets with the theme of 'People who help us' – including a female police officer and an Asian doctor

- a set of jigsaw puzzles showing children helping, which includes a child with special educational needs washing a car

- stories that are not about a child's disability, but in which the lead character just happens to have one.

To weave the thread of diversity throughout your setting, extend this further wherever you have the opportunity. For instance, you can ensure that different styles of clothing are represented in the dressing-up box, and that cooking utensils and food in the home corner (an area that mimics the children's home environment) are representative of the wider world. You can purchase crayons in a range of flesh tones for art activities. There are many possibilities.

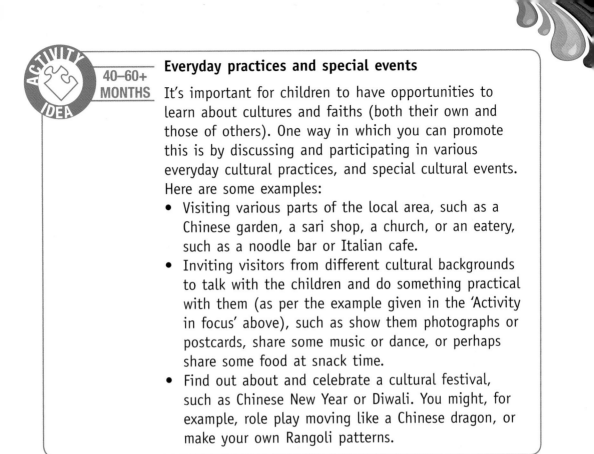

40–60+ MONTHS

Everyday practices and special events

It's important for children to have opportunities to learn about cultures and faiths (both their own and those of others). One way in which you can promote this is by discussing and participating in various everyday cultural practices, and special cultural events. Here are some examples:

- Visiting various parts of the local area, such as a Chinese garden, a sari shop, a church, or an eatery, such as a noodle bar or Italian cafe.
- Inviting visitors from different cultural backgrounds to talk with the children and do something practical with them (as per the example given in the 'Activity in focus' above), such as show them photographs or postcards, share some music or dance, or perhaps share some food at snack time.
- Find out about and celebrate a cultural festival, such as Chinese New Year or Diwali. You might, for example, role play moving like a Chinese dragon, or make your own Rangoli patterns.

❶ Don't forget

It's important that settings avoid tokenism when promoting diversity, inclusion and participation. For instance, you cannot celebrate a festival such as Diwali or the Chinese New Year and then think that you have 'done multi-culturalism' with the children and tick it off your 'to do' list! There's nothing wrong with celebrating festivals as long as that is regarded as just one small way in which children within the setting learn about other cultures. It's the everyday aspects of life that really enable us to learn about another culture, not what people eat and wear once a year on a special occasion. You should also ensure that you use everyday language to present other cultures in a realistic, everyday way. This means you should avoid talking about people and countries in a way that makes them sound exotic or mysterious – it's real people's lives you're talking about, not a fairytale. Avoid making the way other people live their lives sound strange or unusual. Differences should be regarded as commonplace, and you should never value one culture or belief system above another.

Development matters!

Positive relationships: what adults could do

Lennox is a trainee at a children's centre working in a room of 3- and 4-year-olds. His supervisor has asked him to plan an activity that will promote understanding of past events in children's own lives.

The centre has recently expanded to offer provision for babies. Many of the older children have been interested in this, and they have all been to have a look around the new baby room. They often point out what the babies are doing, such as 'Look, the babies are going outside!' or 'Baby Isaac is going home with his daddy ...'. In time, baby room staff plan to bring a few babies along to regularly join the older children for story time or singing, which the group is looking forward to. Lennox decides to use all this interest in babies in his activity.

Lennox plans to read the children a story about a baby – he knows the local library has a copy of the *Baby Brains* series by Simon James. He then plans to talk to the children about when they were younger, and to discuss what they can remember or have been told. He'll then ask each family to bring in a photo of their child when they were a baby or toddler, along with a piece of memorabilia or an artefact (for example, a toy they've had since they were a baby, their first pair of shoes or their old feeder cup). The group can make an interesting table display from these items, which will be a focal point for discussion about how each child has grown and changed throughout their lives.

The world

Early learning goal

The world: Children know about similarities and differences in relation to places, objects, materials and living things. They talk about the features of their own immediate environment and how environments might vary from one another. They make observations of animals and plants, explain why some things occur, and talk about changes.

Activity ideas

Ring the changes

BIRTH–11 MONTHS

Ring the changes in terms of the children's immediate environment and how they experience it. For example, introduce new and interesting moving objects for babies to watch, such as a balloon suspended by an open window, or bubbles floating overhead. Give older babies who enjoy pulling themselves into the standing position the chance to stand on long grass with bare feet and legs – you can encourage them by showing delight at their reaction.

New floor coverings

8–20 MONTHS

Give children a new experience by changing the floor covering beneath them. For example, spread out a large tarpaulin (plastic sheet) that rustles when children move on it or a shiny piece of fabric which feels silky and catches the light, or roll out a long length of paper that can be torn during exploration. Encourage children to interact with the material by hiding favourite objects under the edges.

Development matters!

A unique child: observing what children are learning

Excerpt from a checklist observation of a 10-month-old child showing the development of 'object permanence' (the understanding that something still exists even when it can't be seen) – a key concept in understanding the world.

Activity	Yes	No	Date	Observer's comments
Watches toy being hidden and tries to find it	✔		5/9/12	Shows the toy to an adult when found and takes it to their mouth.
Explores materials/ objects using different approaches	✔		5/9/12	Feels, pulls, twists, pokes and mouths tarpaulin floor covering.

16–26 MONTHS

Heuristic play

Set out a range of different types of object with lids for children to explore in heuristic play, such as saucepans of different sizes, plastic storage jars, cardboard gift boxes.

Extension idea: Provide natural objects to be explored alongside and tipped in and out of the containers, for example pebbles of different colours, textures and sizes.

Development matters!

Positive relationships: what adults could do

Anil works in the toddler room of a day nursery with children in the 16- to 26-month age range. He's been asked to plan an activity that focuses on a range of common animals that the children are familiar with.

Anil decides to ask each parent and carer to bring in a photo of an animal their child knows and likes – this could be their own pet, a creature that visits their garden or an animal that belongs to a neighbour or friend. He plans to make a display of these. He'll then talk about the children's favourite animals, using the display as a focal point. He'll also encourage the children to point out their own animal pictures to visitors to promote further conversation.

Anil also visits the library and selects a range of books featuring familiar animals. He asks each of the key workers to spend some time looking at the books on a one-to-one basis with their key children during the time the display is up.

22–36 MONTHS

Mixing it up

Introduce a small group of children to a mixed-up collection of items that are used in the garden (such as a watering can, a trowel, plant pots) and items that are used at the beach (such as a bucket, a spade, a beach towel). Ask them to help you think about the use of each item and to select which to take on a trip to the beach – the selected items can be packed into a beach bag.

Extension idea: This activity can be extended by making the beach bag of items available for role playing a visit to the beach. Why not place the sand tray on the floor to enhance the experience? You may like to top it up with water and add some shells to create a seabed effect.

Figure 3.19 Children can role play a visit to the beach

ACTIVITY IN FOCUS

30–50 MONTHS

Thirsty flowers

This activity demonstrates how a flower drinks water through its stem.

You will need:
- 3 cut flowers in pale shades – white carnations or pale daffodils work well
- Red and blue food colouring
- 3 jugs of water
- 3 transparent water bottles (to use as vases)
- A funnel
- A spoon
- Aprons for children

What to do:

1. Pass the flowers around a group of children. Encourage them to look at the flowers closely and to talk about them. During the discussion, draw their attention to the fact that the flowers are all the same colour, and ask the children to suggest how the flowers need to be kept in order for them to last for a few days. It's likely that they will suggest putting them in water.

2. Explain to the children that cut flowers drink water through their stems, a bit like through a straw. Because water has no colour, it's difficult for us to see how this happens. But there is a special experiment they can try ...

3. With the children, stir half a bottle of red food colouring into one of the jugs of water. Pour this coloured water into a bottle using the funnel. Put one of the flowers into the bottle and place it somewhere it can be observed but not knocked over, such as a window sill. Repeat this with the blue food colouring and the second flower. Finally, put the third flower into a bottle of plain water.

4. Encourage the children to keep an eye on the flowers throughout the session and to tell you of any changes they notice. Usually, flowers will gradually begin to take on a red or blue tint within two or three hours – the colour will deepen further over time. Talk with the children about the changes they are observing and why they are happening – the flower in the plain water that has not changed colour can be used for comparison.

Extension idea: Red and blue work well as they are strong colours which are easily seen on pale petals. But once children understand how the activity works, they may like to experiment with a range of food colourings – or even try mixing different colours together in one jug – just to see what happens to the petals of their flowers.

Development matters!

A unique child: observing what children are learning

Excerpt from a free description observation of a 3-year-old child who is learning effectively about living things:

… Kai leaves the sand tray and goes to the window sill. He looks at a flower standing in a bottle of coloured water. He points and says, 'It's going blue.' He runs across the room to his key worker. He says, 'See the flower with me!' He takes her hand and leads her to the window sill. She says, 'Oh Kai, look at that! What do you think is happening?' Kai says, 'It's drinking the blue water up this … up this stem.' She says, 'How do you know?' Kai says, 'Because some of its flower is going blue!' He leaves the key worker and runs to the next window sill. He looks closely at a flower standing in plain water …

40–60+ MONTHS

Animal lovers

Give children the opportunity to care for living creatures. Some settings own pets for this purpose, but all settings can undertake activities such as feeding the birds. Encourage children to notice the similarities and differences between the types of bird that visit, providing simple identification books so that children can look up the most common birds that they see and eventually learn to recognise them on sight. You can even make your own identification book, picture cards or displays by taking photos of different types of bird as they visit, labelling them and mounting them in a scrapbook, on stiff card or on a wall display – but make sure the wall is close to the window!

Technology

> ### ⊙ Early learning goal
>
> **Technology:** Children recognise that a range of technology is used in places such as homes and schools. They select and use technology for particular purposes.

Activity ideas

The Development Matters guidance states that the beginnings of understanding technology lie in babies exploring and making sense of objects and how they behave. Specific activities relating to technology are therefore not included for this age range. The development of skills that are the the beginnings of understanding technology are considered in the 'Playing and exploring' and 'Creating and thinking critically' characteristics of effective learning.

16–26 MONTHS

Push the button

Children of this age love to explore toys with features they can press, turn, lift, twist, push or pull and, if in doing so they trigger a mechanism that creates sounds or lights, all the better! They will also be taking notice of everyday technology that does something interesting when an action is taken, such as phones that bleep and ring, cameras which flash and whir, and toasters which pop out toast. So why not build up a collection of toy versions of these pieces of equipment? Not only will children enjoy pressing the buttons and so on, they very soon begin to role play – toddlers can frequently be seen holding a toy phone to their ear, for example. It's an early step towards understanding and using technology equipment for real.

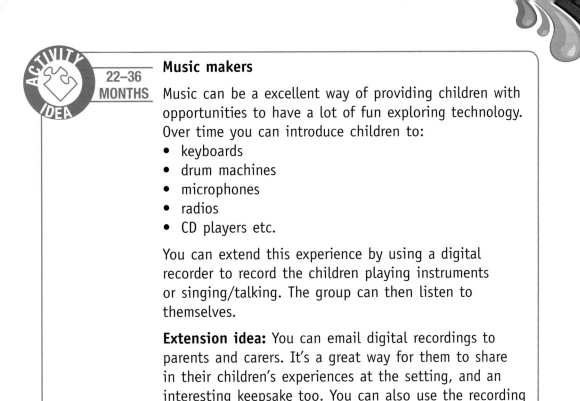

Music makers

ACTIVITY IDEA

22–36 MONTHS

Music can be a excellent way of providing children with opportunities to have a lot of fun exploring technology. Over time you can introduce children to:

- keyboards
- drum machines
- microphones
- radios
- CD players etc.

You can extend this experience by using a digital recorder to record the children playing instruments or singing/talking. The group can then listen to themselves.

Extension idea: You can email digital recordings to parents and carers. It's a great way for them to share in their children's experiences at the setting, and an interesting keepsake too. You can also use the recording for assessment purposes.

Development matters!

A unique child: observing what children are learning

Excerpt from a free description observation of a 2-year-old, Karey, demonstrating how enjoyment of music can promote exploration of technology.

The practitioner (P) sits besides Karey and shows him a keyboard. The volume is switched off. P demonstrates how it lights up when the keys are pressed, then puts it on the carpet. Karey reaches out and places his flat palm on the keys. He watches the lights intently. When the lights stop, he presses the keys again. He repeats twice more, then stands up, leaving the keyboard on the floor. He turns away. P picks it up, turns the volume on and demonstrates what happens now. Karey turns when the notes sound. P repeats her actions. Karey looks on and laughs. He sits down next to P and says 'Me'. P gives him the keyboard.

Take care to ensure that all equipment is safe for children to play with. There may be many things children can do under your close supervision that wouldn't be safe in other circumstances. For example, you may allow them to press the button on the photocopier or the vacuum cleaner, but you wouldn't let them 'play' with these objects.

Walkie-talkies

30–50 MONTHS

Walkie-talkies are another fun use of technology, and there are robust models available for use by this age range. They are enjoyable to simply play with, but why not engage children in using them for real purposes too? For example, you might use them to:

- communicate with children in another room – to invite them to come in and join you for story time perhaps
- communicate with a member of staff in another room – perhaps to tell someone in the kitchen how many children would like milk and how many would like juice at snack time
- communicate with children/staff outside – perhaps to find out how the nursery rabbit is today.

Development matters!

A unique child: observing what children are learning

Excerpt from an observation of a 38-month-old child, Belle, showing an awareness of technology and an interest in operating it:

Belle goes over to a staff member (SM) who is taking a camera from the nursery cupboard. She says, 'Are you taking pictures?' SM says, 'I will after lunch. Do you want to be in one?' Belle nods and says, 'Can I do pressing the button?' SM says, 'You can take a photo if you like, after lunch.' Belle says, 'I want to do one that goes on the computer.'

40–60+ MONTHS

Technology walk

We are surrounded by technology in the modern world. Yet it's very easy to fall into the trap of focusing only on technology children see or play with within the home or the setting. This activity encourages children to recognise everyday technology within the wider community and to understand its purpose.

You will need:
- A camera
- Access to a computer and printer
- A scrapbook and glue pen

What to do:
1. Talk to children about common features of technology, such as things that make sounds, things that light up. Give some examples with which they are very familiar – telephones, for instance, and torches.

2. Now talk about some technological equipment that features in the outside world – such as changing traffic lights, and bleeping pelican crossings.

3. Explain that you are going on a walk to see what technology you can spot. You will take a camera with you, and take a photo of each example you see. (Remember to choose an appropriate route in advance.)

4. On the walk, take the lead in pointing out the features around you, and encourage the children to do the same. Stop and briefly talk about the purpose of the features, for instance, what happens when you press the button at the pelican crossing? What do the cars do when the traffic lights turn red? If you wanted to call on someone who lives in one of the houses, what would you press to let them know you're there? What do people do in a phone box? What happens if you climb on the electronic horse outside the supermarket and put 50p in the slot? Remember to take photos as you go.

5. Later, you can upload the photos to a computer. Children can view them and help to print them out.

6. Mount the photos in a scrapbook and encourage children to show their parents or carers and to tell them all about their walk.

Positive relationships: what adults could do

Kelly is a childminder. She cares part-time for Zack, who is almost 5. Zack is autistic.

Kelly has noticed that Zack shows little interest in operating technology. He's never shown any interest at all in computers, and when she gives him the chance to do things such as pressing a doorbell or operating the CD player to play some music, he often does not want to do it. Zack's parents say he's much the same at home.

Something Zack really loves playing with is his collection of toy cars. He always brings them to Kelly's home. He also likes to look at the books that Kelly provides. It occurs to Kelly that she can use these existing interests to engage Zack with technology. She buys two pull-back-and-go friction cars, and one that can be operated by a simple remote control. She also visits the library and borrows a talking book set, comprising a picture book and a corresponding story recorded on CD.

She plans to introduce the items to Zack gradually over several sessions, as he sometimes finds change unsettling.

Development matters!

Enabling environments: what adults could provide

Older children will be capable of completing simple programs and activities on a computer, but it's important to make sure that software is age appropriate. Always read information carefully before purchasing, and *always* try out all aspects of the software before introducing it to children. (Just like books, software programs can contain inappropriate portrayals of minority groups etc.) Many programs have an additional educational value, such as engaging children in recognising numbers, matching shapes or following a story.

There are also hardware devices which are especially designed for young children. For example, there are simple keyboards with larger buttons and a mouse that fits small hands. This hardware is usually more robust, which means you needn't be constantly nagging children to be more careful than it is realistic to expect.

Expressive arts and design

According to the EYFS framework, expressive arts and design involves enabling children to explore and play with a wide range of media and materials, as well as providing opportunities and encouragement for sharing their thoughts, ideas and feelings through a variety of activities in art, music, movement, dance, role play, and design and technology.

The ELGs

There are two ELGs for this specific area of learning and development:

1. Exploring and using media and materials (see below)

2. Being imaginative (see page 191).

Each one is explained in detail in the relevant section that follows.

Exploring and using media and materials

> ### ◉ Early learning goal
>
> **Exploring and using media and materials**: Children sing songs, make music and dance, and experiment with ways of changing them. They safely use and explore a variety of materials, tools and techniques, experimenting with colour, design, texture, form and function.

Activity ideas

The Development Matters guidance states that babies explore media and materials as part of their exploration of the world around them. Specific activities relating to exploring and using media and materials are therefore not included for this age range. Further information on exploration as a foundation for exploring and using media and materials can be found in the 'Physical development' and 'Understanding the world – The world' sections, and are developed further through the 'Playing and exploring' characteristic of effective learning.

8–26 MONTHS

Sensory exploration – colour, texture and space

Young children thrive on opportunities to explore with their senses, and this activity enables them to experience colour, texture and space through access to a wide range of resources.

You will need:

- A large sheet of plastic or similar to protect the floor
- A large sheet of strong paper – cutting a piece from a large roll of sugar paper is ideal
- Ready-mixed powder paints in a range of colours
- Aprons (where appropriate for the age range)
- A wide range of additional art/craft resources that are suitable for the age group and that include different textures, colours and shapes, such as shredded paper, tissue paper squares, craft confetti, pieces of crepe paper, glue, rice, cellophane shapes, pieces of ribbon and string
- Tools for applying resources, such as paint brushes, glue spreaders and pieces of sponge – younger children will tend to explore with their hands but do also provide other tools

What to do:

1. Prepare the art and craft resources so they are ready for use, for example pour rice into plastic bowls, cut string into pieces.

2. Spread out the plastic sheeting to protect the floor, then spread out the paper. You may need to weight down the corners.

3. Prepare the children by helping them into aprons (where appropriate for the age range). As the children are going to get right onto the paper with the resources, they will get quite messy! Follow your setting's usual procedures on this, for instance babies may just wear their nappies during the activity.

4. Encourage the children to come and explore the paper. Some may like to sit by the edge and tap or poke at it with a hand or foot; others may be keen to be on top of the paper and perhaps make their way across or around it, or sit somewhere in the middle.

5. Place the ready-prepared resources on the paper at different spaced intervals. (Make sure there are some around the edges.) Help children to build the confidence to explore them and to make marks on the paper by demonstrating different ways of handling

the media. You might do some finger painting, for example, or flick or trickle some paint onto the paper with a brush. You can also demonstrate sprinkling on rice, paint powder or sand.

6. Support children by being on hand, and be ready to step in should they try to put resources into their mouths.

7. Allow plenty of time and, if possible, allow the activity to continue for as long as the children are engaged and stimulated by it.

Extension idea: For smaller groups or individuals, within a childminder's setting for example, you might want to consider presenting the activity in a large paddling pool. Doing it this way contains the activity within a particular area and helps to prevent children from feeling overwhelmed by a vast space. It also helps contain any mess created by the activity.

ACTIVITY IDEA

8–26 MONTHS

Sensory exploration

For other activity suggestions related to 'sensory exploration', see the following:

- 'Move to the beat' activity on page 55
- 'New floor coverings' activity on page 173
- 'Heuristic play' activity on page 174.

Development matters!

A unique child: observing what children are learning

Excerpt from a free description observation of a 14-month-old child who is exploring colour and texture.

Leila crawls along the edge of the large sheet of paper. She stops next to a puddle of paint. She sits and pokes it with her index finger. She lays her hand flat and taps the puddle. She looks at her hand. She begins to crawl again but, immediately noticing the handprint she has left, stops and sits back up. She pushes her hand forward on the paper and looks at the smudged paint trail this leaves ...

❗ *Don't forget*

You should always emphasise process over product. This means valuing the creative processes of children ahead of the end product. Creative expression from young children rarely looks 'tidy'. Never be tempted to 'tidy up' children's artwork – this communicates to children that you do not consider their end product to be good enough, and is likely to damage expressive confidence and self-esteem.

22–36 MONTHS

Live performances and art

The chance to see live performances and artists working in the flesh can be hugely inspirational for both young children and practitioners. This includes visual artists (such as painters, collage makers, artists working in textiles), sculptors (working in media, such as wood, clay, metals, plastics), dancers of all genres, musicians (including singers) and actors. Young children's reactions to experiencing live performances and art can go on long after a performance or experience comes to an end, and can be both uplifting and exhilarating. Just imagine being a child seeing and hearing a large, lively choir perform for the first time ...

Try to make connections with artists/performers within the community and to arrange opportunities for children to experience live performances and art in action. There are many ways of achieving this (and it is money well spent):

- Take children to see a professional performance at a live venue
- Visit an artist's studio
- Hire a professional performer(s) (such as a singer or some dancers) to visit the setting.

Other options include:

- inviting members of amateur groups (such as local choirs or amateur dramatics groups) to visit
- seeing community performances which are generally free (a brass band in the park, perhaps).

Guide to the learning and development requirements

It's also good for younger children to see older children engaging in artistic pursuits, and attending performances at local schools can contribute to smoothing the transition to school later.

Make every effort for young children to experience live performances and art, as statistics show that many never experience it with their families. This age is the ideal time to start, but keep the opportunities coming whenever possible.

Extension idea: You may like to take video footage/ photos of the 'live' art experienced by children. This can then be shared and discussed later so the experience can be relived in children's minds. Do make sure you have permission to record artists at work, and be aware that filming and photography are banned in some live venues, such as theatres.

Figure 3.20 The chance to see live performances can be inspirational to children

Imaginative movement

At this age, children are increasingly able to move in imaginative ways when they experience a stimulus that inspires them. You can help children to become inspired with a little creativity of your own.

Music and movement sessions are popular, and you may use some pre-recordings with children. These include a voice-over which typically sets the scene – describing an African savannah, for instance – then guides them to do certain tasks, such as move like a lion to some African music. These types of pre-recordings are available on CD and they are also broadcast on educational radio, and can be of high quality.

Movement opportunities are particularly valuable, however, when they are led by practitioners who know them well and can follow children's interests and respond to the ways they are thinking and moving during the session. The scene can be set in partnership with children, and there can be frequent pauses to talk together and gather children's suggestions. This also provides the opportunity for children's creativity of movement to be inspired by their peers.

Children do not always have to move to music! Others sounds can be evocative and inspirational, such as a CD of rainforest sounds. Children might also want to record their own sounds – how about recording the noise made by traffic in the street, for instance, or the hustle and bustle of a local market, or even the sounds of the seaside? Children can make their own sounds as they move, and there will be times when they move in silence.

Extension idea: You can introduce props, such as ribbons to twirl, during imaginative movement sessions.

Figure 3.21 Music and movement sessions are a popular way of encouraging children to move in imaginative ways

The following resources/equipment can be used to support the exploration of a variety of materials and tools and techniques. They can also be used to promote experimentation:

- Scissors, sticky tape, glue pens, glue sticks
- A diverse range of art and craft resources, including different colours and textures, such as paper, card, tissue, cellophane, paint, glue, felt tips, crayons, craft feathers, lollipop sticks, sequins, buttons, pipe cleaners, wool, string
- Malleable materials, such as play dough, gloop and Plasticine
- Recordings of songs, rhymes and music
- Musical instruments.

Ongoing construction

Children in this age band need time to be creative and expressive – this cannot be rushed. A good example of this is children's construction.

It's good practice to have a well-stocked construction area for children to access freely during most of the time they spend in early years settings. This will include resources such as card, paper, recycled goods (kitchen tubes, boxes, yoghurt pots, various lids, different sized plastic bottles etc.), mark-making materials, joining materials (such as glue and sticky-tape), tools (such as scissors). It will also include manufactured construction materials, such as blocks and interlocking bricks.

However, an important aspect of construction which is often overlooked is providing children with the opportunity to revisit their constructions over a period of time, so don't be in too much of a hurry to send children's recycled models home or to dismantle constructions at tidy-up time. Instead, give children the freedom to rework them and to add to them, and to develop a continuing train of construction thought and practice.

Also, why not try reintroducing children's constructions in a new way. For example, if you introduce malleable materials to the construction area and make a child's previously made recycled model available alongside, a child may mesh together two materials they wouldn't otherwise have combined, and turn their previous creation into something new. Or, you might try changing locations by taking previous constructions outside.

Development matters!

Being imaginative

◎ Early learning goal

Being imaginative: Children use what they have learned about media and materials in original ways, thinking about uses and purposes. They represent their own ideas, thoughts and feelings through design and technology, art, music, dance, role play and stories.

Activity ideas

As stated in the Development Matters guidance, babies and toddlers need to explore the world and develop a range of ways to communicate before they can express their own ideas through arts and design. Specific activities relating to being imaginative are therefore not included for this age range. Further information on the development of skills that are the foundation of being imaginative can be found in the 'Communication and language', 'Physical development' and 'Personal, social and emotional development' sections, and developed through the different characteristics of effective learning.

Imagine this

At this age children are just starting to pretend and engage in imaginative play. You can support this by providing access to play resources that reflect the real world children see around them every day. A home corner is an early years staple – most children will be familiar with mealtime resources (a cooker, saucepans, plates, cutlery etc.) and items such as telephones, and this familiarity helps them to create pretend scenarios, such as 'the dinner being ready'.

Always appreciate children's early pretend play and treat it with sensitivity. Show interest and play along when children involve you, perhaps by bringing you a 'cup of tea', or by pretending there's someone who wants to speak to you on the phone.

It's important to let children take the lead in imaginary play. However, the children in this age range will need support and suggestions to help them to extend and develop their pretending. You can provide this by modelling pretend play rather than giving the child instructions. You might say, 'I think I can hear the phone ringing again …' rather than, 'Call your mummy on the phone'.

Figure 3.22 A home corner supports imaginative play

A unique child: observing what children are learning

Excerpt from a free description observation of a 24-month-old child which demonstrates a practitioner effectively modelling an imaginative idea which is taken up by a child and incorporated into their play.

> Denzel is playing in the home corner with his peer, Saffron. A practitioner (P) is nearby. Denzel finds a saucepan of pasta on the cooker. He says to P, 'Pasta'. P says, 'Is there pasta cooking in the saucepan? Lovely! I like cooking pasta. I give it a good stir.' Denzel fetches a wooden spoon from the kitchen drawer. He takes it to the cooker and uses it to stir the pasta ...

❗ Don't forget

One of the most effective and powerful ways for you to promote being imaginative is to ensure that children see you being creative and using creative thinking skills within the setting. The goal is to model techniques rather than to give children prescriptive instructions which could hamper their imaginative development and undermine their confidence. So you may paint your own picture alongside a child, for instance, using the paintbrush in a dabbing motion to allow a child to see a different way of mark making, which they can try for themselves if they want to.

ACTIVITY IN FOCUS

22–55 MONTHS

Creative processes

At this age, children are increasingly able to talk about the ideas behind their creative processes, and they will also be starting to use representation to communicate meaning – for instance, they may make a blob with some paint and say, 'There's daddy.'

1. You can encourage this and help to give children language to express their creative processes by playing alongside them and

voicing your own creative processes. For example, share a story, such as *Handa's Surprise*, with a small group of children to set an imaginary scene.

2. Introduce props that represent elements of the story and make them available for play, such as puppets, an assortment of fruit and various baskets.

3. Give children a chance to explore the objects, and have their own creative thoughts and talk about them.

4. Play alongside children and provide a commentary of your creative processes, for example 'I think I'll call this puppet Handa. She's walking along ... I wonder where she's going? I know, she wants to buy some fruit, so she'll go to the market ...'

5. Take a note of the impact this has on the children's play and respond when appropriate.

6. Model new thought processes and provide further commentary should children's play begin to flag.

This activity demonstrates that you value children's thought processes, that they are worth sharing with others and that you are happy to play along with imaginative play.

Extension idea: You can also make up stories based on children's experiences, and the people and places they are familiar with, instead of drawing inspiration from a book.

Development matters!

Enabling environments: what adults could provide

Provide children extended, unhurried periods of time to be imaginative within their environment. Expression, imagination and creative learning cannot be rushed. Imaginative ideas and insights take time to develop. When children first participate in an activity or experience, they are likely to do something familiar, something they have done before. They need extended, unhurried periods to really get into activities and experiences, and to engage at a deeper level. This is when new connections, and new explorations and discoveries tend to be made.

Time is also important when it comes to creating new ideas. Often, children (and adults) will only begin to think creatively once all the obvious suggestions have been made, or all the most common ways of doing something have been tried. It takes time to work through all of these and to move into the deeper, richer, more imaginative stuff.

Ask Miranda!

Q: Won't children become bored if activities aren't changing frequently?

A: Young children will be accessing expressive activities and experiences as part of their free play, so opportunities to engage for extended periods will be offered within an environment that also facilitates moving on to the next thing when children are ready. In fact, an important part of making creative connections for young children is joining and mixing up what is on offer to them – taking some water to the sand tray, for instance, or taking a car to the drawing table and subsequently drawing a road.

ACTIVITY IDEA

40–60+ MONTHS

Guided story solutions

In this activity you will make up the beginnings of a story and present it to children as an event which is happening here and now. The story should contain some sort of problem for children to solve. This will pull them into the event, and how they decide to respond will shape the rest of the unfolding story. A full example is given in the following Development matters! feature. Why not use this example the first time you try this activity, and see where the children take the story? The next time, you can make up your own problem or incident. It is important to get colleagues to engage in the activity.

Development matters!

Positive relationships: what adults could do

While the children are visiting the baby room to share some songs with their younger peers, practitioner Carla places a large sealed cardboard box on the rug. The children notice it immediately when they return. Several want to know what's inside.

Carla says, 'I don't know, I hadn't noticed it there before. Does it belong to any of you?' The children indicate 'no'. Carla says, 'I wonder how it got there?'

❗ Don't forget

When children respond to the activities and experiences that you provide with wonder and excitement, this often indicates that creativity and/or expression is taking place. Different children will be drawn to different aspects of creativity and imagination, and it is part of a practitioner's role to not only help children experience a full range of opportunities, but also to help them find what excites them and gives them that expressive, imaginative spark.

4 Assessment and planning

Assessment

What is assessment?

The EYFS framework tells us that ongoing assessment by practitioners is integral (central) to children's learning and development. Assessment involves the observation of children by practitioners to understand:

- **Their level of achievement:** the things a child can currently do in each area of their development, such as kicking a ball, speaking in full sentences, taking turns during a game.

- **Their interests:** the things a child is interested in and the things they like to do, such as finding out about animals, dancing, building things, sharing stories.

- **Their learning styles:** the ways in which a child learns particularly well, for example, through discussion and listening (auditory learners), through seeing and imagining (visual learners), and through experiencing/active learning (kinaesthetic learners). Further details are included on page 225.

Involving parents and carers in assessment

- In addition to making their own observations, practitioners should reflect on the observations shared by a child's parents or primary carers. It's important to remember that parents generally know their child best. They often have insight into progress that you may never directly observe – a child learning to swim, for example. It's also likely that a child will show interest in different things outside the early years setting.

- It's important for practitioners to share their assessments with a child's parents and carers – you'll learn more about this on pages 237–242.

Ask Miranda!

Q: I'm concerned that I can't tell which style of learning best suits some children. What types of learning opportunity should I provide for them?

A: Don't be deceived by the learning styles! While many adults and children may have a preferred way of learning, we can all learn effectively in different ways. In particular it's important to remember that *all* children are active learners through play and doing things, and that *all* young children need diverse experiences. It's far better to provide a balanced choice of learning opportunities across the styles than to limit children's opportunities by selecting the way they learn. Also, remember that young children are inexperienced learners, and their preferred learning style will emerge slowly and even change over time as they develop and respond to new experiences. You can read more about learning styles on page 225.

Figure 4.1 All children are active learners

The purpose of assessment within the EYFS

The EYFS framework tells us that assessment plays an important part in helping parents, carers and practitioners to:

- recognise children's progress
- understand children's needs and development
- plan activities and support for children.

We'll look at each of these in turn during this part of the book.

Recognising children's progress

- Young children learn and develop constantly and rapidly in the early years. So when you observe a child you can only ever capture a snapshot of their development at that particular moment. By observing children regularly, however, you can build an overview of how their development is progressing over time. This is often referred to as 'tracking development', and is an important part of assessment.

Ask Miranda!

Q: How much do I need to know about child development to assess children's progress well?

A: A good general knowledge and understanding of child development is needed by all practitioners as this is at the heart of effective assessment.

In addition to the Development Matters guidance, there are many books dedicated to the subject of child development, and you are advised to read widely. It's important to keep your knowledge up to date as we are discovering more about how children learn all the time. For example, in recent years neuroscientists have been able to study children's brains as they play. This has taught us much about the types of connection that are made in the brain as children learn and think.

Understanding children's needs and development

By tracking development, practitioners with a good general knowledge of child development can better understand an individual child's needs. They will be able to identify:

- the skills a child has already developed and the learning a child has already achieved

- the skills and learning a child is currently consolidating (strengthening through practice or repeated experience, such as writing their own name)

- the skills and learning a child is likely to develop or achieve next (for example, a 1-year-old baby who stands on their own may soon be ready to walk)

- whether a child is experiencing difficulties in any areas of their learning and development.

How do practitioners go about understanding children's development?

As part of an effective assessment process, practitioners will compare a child's current stage of development (the skills and learning they have achieved) with the expected development patterns for a child of their age. This helps practitioners to identify when development is not occurring as usually expected. This in turn may indicate that a child is experiencing difficulty in one or more areas of their learning and development.

The importance of identifying when development is not occurring as expected

It's important that practitioners identify when development is not occurring as expected as a child may need support or intervention to:

- pinpoint the cause of the difficulty
- identify and meet their learning and development needs.

The quicker the above can be achieved the better it is, for both the child's welfare and their ongoing development. Some children experience difficulties which can be completely overcome with the right support. For example:

- A child may struggle to piece together jigsaw puzzles but may soon get the hang of it with targeted adult support and plenty of opportunities to play with puzzle sets
- Some speech difficulties fade away entirely with speech and language therapy.

Some children experience difficulties that affect them for a longer period or on a permanent basis, but the effect of these may be limited with the use of special equipment or a particular approach – the use of a hearing aid, for example, or learning Makaton (a basic sign language used with younger children and those with learning difficulties, which enables more effective communication).

❗ Don't forget

As you learned in Part 3 of this book, children do develop at different rates. This is normal and should be anticipated. Development patterns or milestones are only ever approximate – that's why the age bands overlap in the Development Matters guidance. But a significant delay in one area of development or a number of delays in more than one area is a concern, and action should be taken in line with the policies and procedures at your setting. Usually, this will involve the child's key worker consulting with the setting's Special Educational Needs Coordinator (SENCO) and arranging a time to discuss the assessment findings with the child's parent or carer. It may then be appropriate to seek the help of professionals outside the setting. (For example, the child may see their GP and be referred to a speech and language therapist.) There is further information about this on pages 259–260.

Comparing a child's current stage of development against the expected sequence also makes it possible for practitioners to predict what a child is likely to learn next. This informs the planning process by enabling practitioners to provide activities and experiences that will promote the next phase of the child's learning and development. For example, if a practitioner knows that a 1-year-old who stands on their own is likely to begin walking soon, they might provide plenty of floor space and a push-along baby walker to promote that skill.

Figure 4.2 A 1-year-old who stands on their own is likely to begin walking soon

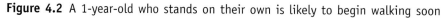

Is there a resource to help me with understanding development patterns?

You can use the non-statutory Development Matters guidance to look up the expected development patterns for children in the early years. This will help you to identify both how children are likely to learn and develop next, and whether a child is experiencing difficulty with one or more areas of their development. (See Parts 2 and 3 of this book for further information about using the Developing Matters guidance.) The Development Matters guidance also provides planning suggestions for children at each stage of their development.

! Don't forget

Children generally develop in broadly the same sequence. For example, babies will learn to roll over before they sit up, and children will say single words before they string two or three together in early sentences. There are, however, exceptions. For instance, children with disabilities may have a specific need and will be expected to develop differently. This should be considered during assessment and planning. There is further information about this on pages 259–260.

Ask Miranda!

Q: When planning activities, how might a practitioner take into consideration the fact that a particular child is expected to develop differently?

A: Here's a brief example to illustrate how this might be done. Tansy, who is 4, has cerebral palsy and uses a wheelchair. Her large motor skills are affected, and doctors don't expect her to stand, walk or crawl at any time during her life. But there are other ways in which she can travel. She's currently learning to roll across the floor at nursery. And when she goes to the swimming pool, Tansy floats on her back with minimal help from her dad. She's expected to float alone before too long. While she does experience difficulty with her fine motor skills, her hospital consultant says it's likely that Tansy will be able to increase her finger dexterity in time, enabling her eventually to operate an electric wheelchair safely and experience more independence. This is an important goal for Tansy. Her key worker plans a variety of engaging activities to promote Tansy's fine motor skills. As Tansy particularly enjoys artistic activities, she is given opportunities to make her mark in various ways as this encourages her to manipulate with her hands, fingers and thumbs.

Planning activities and support for children

Please see pages 216–234 of this book where this is covered in detail.

EYFS guidance on carrying out ongoing assessment

The previous EYFS framework was not prescriptive about the way in which ongoing assessment should be carried out, so settings were free to adopt their own methods and procedures. While this was generally desirable, a lack of clarity on what was required led to concerns being raised about some practitioners spending excessive time on the assessment process. The concerns related to how frequently and how long they were engaged in conducting formal observations, which often prevent normal interaction between adults and children. There were also concerns about the amount of time spent completing lengthy assessment paperwork. Both issues have been addressed in the revised EYFS framework. There is still no prescribed way in which to carry out ongoing assessment, but the framework clearly states that assessment should not:

- entail prolonged breaks from interaction with children

- require excessive paperwork. Paperwork should be limited to that which is absolutely necessary to promote children's successful learning and development.

The assessment cycle

To be effective, assessment must occur in an ongoing cycle, as the diagram below shows:

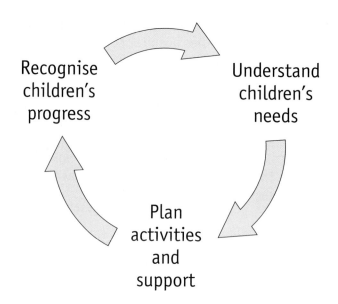

Figure 4.3 The assessment cycle

Assessment and planning

Ask Miranda!

Q: So why do we need each phase in the assessment cycle?

A: We need to continually recognise the progress made by individual children because they learn and develop rapidly in the early years. Up-to-date information about a child's progress enables us to understand their changing needs. We can then respond by planning relevant activities and support. This impacts on the ongoing progress the child makes, and so the whole cycle begins again.

Methods of assessment

There are various methods of assessment which we will go into below but, essentially, practitioners make observations of the children they work with, noticing the things they can do. Some of the observations will be:

- mental notes – accumulated as they work with the children on a daily basis

- written notes – recorded at a planned time the practitioner has dedicated to observing a particular child's behaviour.

❗ Don't forget

These observations should not entail prolonged breaks from interaction with children or require excessive paperwork.

In addition, some knowledge may have been gained from seeing children's work products (such as drawings), or through conversation with parents, carers, colleagues or other professionals. All these things provide evidence of a child's achievements, and knowledge of them is collected over time.

A range of written observation methods that can be used is described on the following pages. An important part of a practitioner's role is to select an observation method that is appropriate to the:

- type of information that they want to collect

- purpose for which the information will be used

- policies and procedures in place at their setting

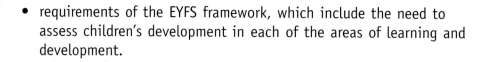

- requirements of the EYFS framework, which include the need to assess children's development in each of the areas of learning and development.

> **⚠ Don't forget**
> --
>
> Using a selection of observation methods over a period of time helps to build up a differentiated (varied) picture of a child's learning and development.

> **⚠ Don't forget**
> --
>
> Practitioners must plan their observation time with colleagues to ensure that it fits in with the overall plans of the setting. Bear in mind that, when carrying out an observation, it may be necessary to abandon it in response to a situation in the room. For example, you may see something unsafe about to happen or you may need to attend to a child in search of assistance if other practitioners are busy. Children's immediate needs should always come first.

Whatever method of observation is used, the following key pieces of information are always needed:

- name of the child (or alternative method of identifying them – initials perhaps)
- date and timing of the observation
- where the observation was carried out
- name of the observer
- activity observed or objective of the observation
- other children present
- other adults present.

The presentation of observation records differs from setting to setting. The key methods of observation are outlined as follows.

Diary

Some settings use a diary system to briefly record what children do on a daily basis. Often the diary is shared with parents and carers, and goes back and forth each day between the home and the setting. This is especially useful for children who cannot tell their parents about their experiences themselves, such as babies, younger children and those with learning or communication difficulties. The diary is generally completed by a child's key worker. Parents may write in the diary to inform practitioners about the child's experiences at home, and to comment on the practitioner's entries. This makes the diary a useful way to build positive relationships and work in partnership with parents and carers.

You will need:

- a diary
- a pen.

What to do

At the end of a session, make a note of the key things the child did, and of anything else you think is important. For example, for a baby you would record:

- when they slept and for how long
- when they had a nappy changed and whether they were wet or dirty
- when they were fed and how much feed they took
- experiences they enjoyed, for example, they clapped hands during a sing song.

As young children grow up, the diary will begin to focus more on the activities they've taken part in and less on how their care needs were met.

> **❗ Don't forget**
>
> - Some practitioners call the diary that is passed between the home and the setting a 'contact book'. Some settings may include photos within the diary.

Narrative observation

The observer focuses on the activity of the child, writing down everything seen during the allotted time. Narrative observations are generally short, lasting for perhaps five minutes or less. They are helpful for focusing on particular areas of difficulty, for instance, working out exactly what is happening when a child struggles to feed themselves. These observations are often recorded in a notebook and written up afterwards.

You will need:

- a notepad
- a pen.

What to do

Write a detailed description of how the child carries out the activity being observed.

Note their actions and behaviour, including their facial expressions. Record what the child says and any non-verbal communication, such as gestures. This is intensive work, which is why it is generally done for just a few minutes. Observations are usually recorded in the present tense, for example – Ben is sitting at the painting table next to Jessica. He picks up his paintbrush and looks at her. She looks back. He smiles and holds his brush out to her. Jessica takes it and smiles back. Ben says, 'Thank you'.

> **❗ Don't forget**
>
> Some practitioners call the narrative observation method 'free description'.

Running records

Running records are a variation on narrative records. Practitioners record all they see as before, but the timing depends on what is happening in the setting rather than being fixed beforehand. For example, you may record a short 'snapshot' of something interesting a child is doing, or everything that takes place at the water tray for a set amount of time. This type of observation is useful because it enables practitioners to assess how effective their activities are by focusing closely on how children experience them.

You will need:

- a notepad
- a pen.

What to do

Record all you see – but be flexible in the timing. For example, if you are responding to something interesting a child is doing, note their actions and behaviour, including their facial expressions. Record what they say and any non-verbal communication, such as gestures.

Figure 4.4 Running records can be used to observe an activity

Time sampling

The observer decides on a period of time for the observation, perhaps two hours. The child's activity is recorded on a form at set intervals – perhaps every 15 minutes. Significant behaviours may occur between the intervals, however, and these will not be recorded.

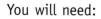

You will need:

- a prepared form giving the times for the observations
- a pen
- a watch.

What to do

Keep an eye on the time to ensure you observe at regular intervals. At each allotted time, observe the child and record their activity in the same way as in the 'narrative' observation.

For example:

10.00am: Ben is sitting at the painting table next to Jessica. He picks up his paintbrush and looks at her. She looks back. He smiles and holds his brush out to her. Jessica takes it and smiles back. Ben says, 'Thank you'.

10.15am: Ben gets down from the table. He goes to the nursery nurse. He looks at her and says, 'Wash hands'.

Event recording

This method is used when practitioners have a reason to record how often an aspect of a child's behaviour or development occurs. For example, practitioners may want to observe how frequently a child is physically aggressive, as shown in the event recording table on the next page. A form is prepared identifying the aspect being tracked. Each time the behaviour or development occurs, a note of the time and circumstance is recorded. Observations may take place over a session, a week or, in some circumstances, longer.

You will need:

- a prepared form adapted for the objective of the observation
- a pen.

What to do

Observe a child, and each time the aspect of behaviour or development of interest occurs, record the circumstances along with the time, as in the example that follows.

Event no.	Time	Event	Circumstances
1	2.30pm	Joshua pushed Daisy over	Joshua had left his teddy on the floor. He watched Daisy pick it up. He went over to Daisy and tried to take the teddy. She did not let go. Joshua pushed her over. Daisy gave Joshua the toy and started to cry. Joshua walked away quickly with the teddy

Figure 4.5 An event recording table

Checklist observation

A form prompts the observer to look for particular skills or reflexes that a child has. The observer ticks them off as they are seen. This method is frequently used for assessing a child's stage of development. It is well suited to the observation of babies, whose physical development will typically progress rapidly. The observations may be made over time, or babies and children may be asked to carry out specific tasks.

You will need:

- a prepared checklist (these can be purchased or developed by practitioners)

- a pen.

What to do

The checklist prompts what you should observe and record (see below). If you are a participant observer, encourage the child to carry out the necessary tasks, and tick the relevant boxes to record their response – generally whether they could carry out the task competently. If you are a non-participant observer, tick the boxes as you see evidence of the child's competence naturally occurring. (You will learn more about participant/non-participant observers on pages 214–215.)

Activity	Yes	No	Date	Observer's comments
Rolls from back to front				

Figure 4.6 An observation checklist

> **❗ Don't forget**
>
> Some practitioners call the checklist observation method 'tick list' observation.

Target child observation

The observer records a child's activity over a long period of time but, unlike the time sampling method, there are no gaps during the observation. To achieve this, the observer uses a range of abbreviations or codes to record what is happening on a ready-prepared form.

You will need:

- a prepared form, with a key to the abbreviations that will be used
- a pen
- a watch.

What to do

It is impossible to record everything a child does over a long period so, with this type of observation, the practitioner must decide which things are significant enough to be noted. (It is interesting to consider what happens when two people observe the same target child over the same period and then compare their forms. They are likely to have recorded different things.) Language and activity are noted in separate columns for ease. It takes practice to get used to using the abbreviations. For example:

Time	Activity	Language	Social grouping	Involvement Level
11.30 am	TC goes to the box of blocks. Uses both hands to tip the box up and get the blocks out	_TC_ 'Out'	SOL	1
11.31 am	TC sits down. Using right hand he places one block on top of another. He repeats this, building a tower of four blocks		SOL	1

Key:

TC	= target child
_TC_	= target child talking to self
SOL	= solitary grouping
1	= target child absorbed in their activity

Additional codes will be used, and codes vary within settings.

Figure 4.7 A target child observation form

Anecdotal records

Anecdotal records are made when a practitioner is told by someone else about something important or interesting the child has done. For example, a child's parent or carer or another practitioner may tell you that they have seen a child crawl for the first time, or that the child has said their first sentence. This anecdotal information can be added in note form to a child's development records. The date and the name of the person who observed the occurrence should also be recorded.

Photos, film clips, audio clips

These can provide a helpful record of children's activities. Photos are useful for recording things a child has created that can't usually be saved – a sand sculpture, for instance, or a Lego creation. In the case of film, more information than it's possible to put on paper can be recorded with complete accuracy. There's also the advantage of replaying it to ensure nothing is missed, and showing it to parents, carers, colleagues, other professionals and the child or young person for discussion. Audio clips can be used in a similar way and are particularly well suited to recording language development. Ensure you have permission, for *all* children present, to record assessments in these ways as other children may wander into range and also be recorded.

Observation with or without adults

When children play on their own or with their peers, they may behave quite differently from when there is an adult joining in with them. So observers need to decide whether they want to observe a child with or without direct interaction from other adults. Ideally, children will be observed both with and without adults over a period of time.

During observations, the behaviour of children can change. If they are aware of being watched, some children feel anxious or excited, or they may try harder than usual. To counteract this, the practitioner may decide to be a 'non-participant observer'.

Non-participant observers

Non-participant observers are unobtrusive – they settle themselves somewhere suitable to watch the children without alerting them to the fact they are being observed. The observer does not speak or interact with the children during this time. There is therefore no need to make a record of their own actions or words during the observation.

It's easier to be objective and to record what is happening when you are not involved in events. It can be difficult, however, to find somewhere unobtrusive that still allows you to see and hear everything that occurs. As a non-participant observer, it is possible to use any method of observation, but this technique is well suited to the 'narrative' and 'target child' methods.

Figure 4.8 A participant observer can encourage children to carry out the necessary tasks

Participant observers

'Participant observers' can directly ask or encourage children to do things, which is advantageous if you are looking to record particular aspects of development or behaviour. This technique works well with the 'checklist' method of observation. Participant observers can also ask questions to find out the reason for a child's behaviour – 'Why are you doing that?'

Assessing and evaluating observations

Once an observation (or series of observations) has been completed, a practitioner will consider the observation carefully and then draw conclusions. The consideration aspect is often known as 'observation assessment', and the conclusions drawn are known as the 'evaluation' or the 'outcome'. Some people refer to the whole process of assessing and evaluating as the 'interpretation'.

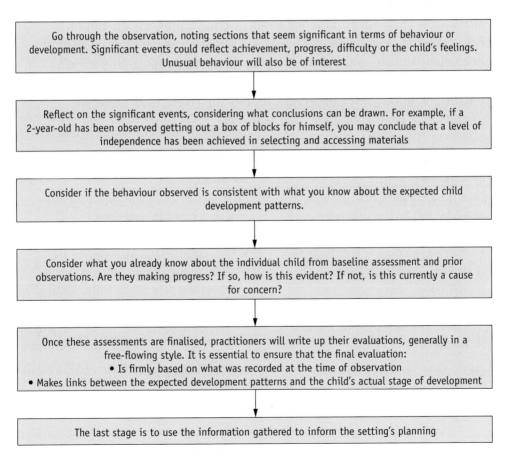

Figure 4.9 A common procedure for assessing and evaluating observations

Settings will have developed their own techniques for interpretation and for the way in which the interpretation is presented in written format. You should follow your setting's guidelines. Generally speaking, however, practitioners will follow a procedure similar to the one outlined in the table below.

> ❗ **Don't forget**
> --
>
> The EYFS framework says that, 'In their interactions with children, practitioners should respond to their own day-to-day observations about children's progress, and observations that parents and carers share'.

Planning activities and support for children

Once interpretations have been made, practitioners must use the information they have gathered about a child's progress to inform their planning. Practitioners should ask themselves, 'In the light of the conclusions drawn, what should I plan to do to support this child's future progress and learning?' The table below shows some possible conclusions drawn from observation, and the likely next steps in supporting a child's progress and learning.

Possible conclusion drawn from observation	Next step in supporting progress and learning
Child is having difficulties learning a particular skill and/or understanding a certain concept, for example: • they may be finding it difficult to acquire a skill, such as the use of scissors • they may find it difficult to follow stories and have little idea of how to handle books.	Extra support or learning opportunities may be planned to help them. For example: • Provide more opportunities for the child to use scissors, such as cutting string and play dough (with plastic scissors) • Provide opportunities for the child to share books on a one-to-one basis with an adult.

Possible conclusion drawn from observation	Next step in supporting progress and learning
Child has particular, persistent difficulties in one or more areas of their learning or development, such as: • they have a special educational need • they have missed learning opportunities due to a period of illness • they are bilingual or multilingual and are learning the home language of the setting.	• Practitioners should already be receiving support from outside professionals and agencies, and an Individual Education Plan (IEP) may already be in place. If so, practitioners should consider the child's progress towards curriculum requirements and their IEP since the last assessment. • *If progress is being made*, practitioners should consider what children should learn next in the light of their current development. • *If sufficient progress is not being made*, practitioners can, in consultation with families, refer back to outside professionals and agencies for advice and support. If the difficulties are unexpected, practitioners should work in consultation with colleagues, families and, where appropriate, children to try to identify the cause. Then children can be given the right support. • Outside professionals and external agencies should be contacted if necessary (again in consultation) if practitioners suspect that a child has an impairment or special educational need. There is further information about this on pages 259–260.

Child is progressing well	• Practitioners should plan for continued progress.
	• Practitioners should consider what the child should learn next:
	  – What is the next step of their development?
	  – What opportunities should be provided for them?
	  – What support may they need to continue their progress?
	• Reference to the Development Matters guidance can be helpful at this stage.

Figure 4.10 A child may benefit from opportunities to share books on a one-to-one basis with an adult

❗ Don't forget

The EYFS framework requires practitioners to use the information they gather through observation to shape the learning experiences for each child in their care.

The planning cycle

The planning cycle has three parts:

1. Planning for learning and development
2. Implementing opportunities for learning and development
3. Reviewing and evaluating learning and development.

The process of reviewing and evaluating informs the next planning session, and so the cycle begins again.

Planning activities and experiences

Practitioners must plan how they will provide activities and experiences that will promote children's learning and development, and help them to progress towards the early learning goals in each area of learning and development. Planning enables practitioners to ensure that the learning environment is:

- purposeful
- supportive
- challenging
- varied
- balanced
- vibrant and exciting.

Purposeful

Play and activities should benefit children in terms of learning and experience. (Don't forget that having fun is an experience!)

Supportive

Activities and play are planned with regard to the support that individual children may need. They are also devised with children's sense of confidence, self-esteem and general well-being in mind.

Challenging

Opportunities that challenge children are offered as well as those that consolidate learning. This encourages motivation and progression in terms of learning.

Varied

There should be planned, adult-led activities as well as free-play and child-initiated activities. Learning should take place both indoors and outside. A range of physically active pursuits should be offered as well as those that require quiet concentration.

Balanced

Opportunities should be provided to stimulate children's learning in all areas of their development and learning, and they should appeal to different styles of learner (see page 225).

Vibrant and exciting

Interesting, exciting activities motivate children. They help to foster a love of learning and discovery.

Long-term, medium-term and short-term planning

Practitioners generally make plans to show how learning will take place in the:

- long term
- medium term
- short term.

Most practitioners approach this by planning for the long term first, then the medium term and lastly the short term.

Making and recording long-term, medium-term and short-term plans

There are many good ways to make and record plans. Examples are given here, but it's important that you follow your setting's requirements when drawing up your own plans.

	SEP	OCT	NOV	DEC	JAN	FEB	MAR	APR	MAY	JUN	JUL	AUG
Theme	Autumn	Animals	Light	Patterns	Winter	Story time	Health	Spring in the garden	Carnival	Summer holidays	Sport	Our home
Special events and activities	Trip to country park	Visits to children's farm	Diwali visit to Hindu temple	Visit from artist Christmas	Parents' evening	Visit from African storyteller	Visits from a dentist and a doctor	Trip to garden centre	Fancy dress party	Picnic by the sea	Sports open day	Family barbecue
C&L												
PD												
PSED												
L												
M												
UtW												
EA&D												

The ELGs to be promoted by each special event or activity will be entered in the table. Settings often number the ELGs according to the order in which they're listed in the EYFS framework, so that they can be identified easily in the plans. For example, if the ELG 'People and communities' is being promoted, they may enter 'UtW 1'or if the ELG 'Technology' is being promoted, they may enter 'UtW 3'.

Key

C&L: Communication and language; PD: Physical development; PSED: Personal, social and emotional development;

L: Literacy; M: Mathematics; UtW: Understanding the world; EA&D: Expressive arts and design.

Figure 4.11 An example of long-term planning

THEME: My body	DATE: October 1st–5th	ROOM: Rainbows	AGE RANGE: 3–5 years	PLANNED BY: Sonia B. and Clare S.	EVALUATION NOTES BY:
	Learning intentions for children based on ELGs	Activities and play experiences	Assessment: how we will know what individuals have learned	Specific support to be provided for individual children	Evaluation notes to inform future planning (This section to be completed at the end of the session).
Communication and language	Children listen attentively to stories and answer 'how' and 'why' questions.	Story book *My House* at story time, then discuss what shelter is and why we need it in the form of homes, e.g. what would happen if we didn't have a roof? And what sort of different homes are there? (e.g. houses, flats, caravans, barges, bungalows etc).	Take note of significant comments made by individual children and level of engagement during story.	Support GT by using the key Italian words for different types of homes: check these with his Dad beforehand.	
Physical development	Understanding that physical activity is good for us, recognising/ responding to changes in our bodies.	Group discussion after a lively game of 'Traffic Lights' (in which children start and stop their body movements): how are our bodies feeling: are we hot? Tired? Can we feel our hearts beating? Are we thirsty? What might we need? (E.g. a drink, a short rest). Why was the physical activity good for us?	Take note of significant comments made by individual children.	Gently encourage SL to speak up within the group.	
Personal, social and emotional development	Children develop confidence to try new activities, share their ideas and choose the resources they need for selected activities.	Imaginary area 1 to be a hairdressers, area 2 to be a dentist's surgery. Children to choose what they need to set up these areas from a diverse range of props.	Take note of individuals' roles in choosing resources/ props provided, and the use of these in play. Is imaginary play co-operative?		
Literacy	Children use phonics to decode regular words and read them aloud, and they also use phonics to write simple words.	Decide on body captions needed for the children's person collage (already displayed on the large pin board). Make captions on computer together, sounding out phonics. (Captions to go in the word bank when the display is removed).	Take note of individual children's phonetic use and their contributions to finding letters on the keyboard.		
Mathematics	Children count and participate in solving problems including sharing out.	Sharing out fruit and a jug of milk for a healthy snack: how many of us are there? How many pieces of fruit can we have each? How many cups will we need? How many will we have left? etc	Take note of how effectively individuals are counting and following number operations.	TS will need her adapted knife and non-slip table mat when slicing bananas etc.	
Understanding the world	Understanding and describing similarities/differences in objects, living things and the features around them.	Feely bag game utilising touch, smell, hearing and (on the reveal) sight. Objects to include plants, fruit, veg. (Could extend with a tasting of the fruit/veg).	Take note of individuals' comments and significant reactions to using each of their senses.		
Expressive arts and design	Children select and use range of materials in original ways, thinking about uses and purposes. They represent their thoughts and feelings through design and technology, and role play.	Making our own shelters (dens) from fabric and choice of other materials. (Activity to follow discussion about houses and homes: see Communication and language).	Take note of individuals' comments and use of materials.		

Figure 4.12 An example of short-term planning

Deciding how to plan

The short-term planning example shows that a theme has been selected. While it's generally agreed that themes are not beneficial for children under 2½ years of age, many settings do find them effective for older children. They can be a good way to link activities and play experiences, making them purposeful and progressive. The table below shows how a group of practitioners may plan a theme for a setting following the EYFS framework.

Step one
Take a theme and set a timescale, e.g. gardening, two weeks (this may be informed by the long-term plan). Let parents and carers know the theme and encourage them to become involved – with planning ideas, or collecting resources perhaps.
Step two
Divide the theme into subcategories, identifying a logical order for progressive learning, e.g. planting, growing etc.
Step three
Referring to the aspects within the areas of learning, plan activities and play for children's learning, related to the theme. Take account of individual children's needs, play plans and individual learning styles. Plan a balance of activities and play across the curriculum, for all areas of learning.
Step four
Take the activities and play opportunities identified, and fit them into a timetable for each week, around the normal routines such as circle time and snack time. Ensure variation between the types of activities to keep children interested and to give time for being active as well as time for them to rest and recharge their batteries, taking children's attendance patterns into consideration.
Step five
Identify the roles of adults. Who will do what, and how should children be generally supported? What resources/equipment are needed, and who will organise them?
Step six
Identify opportunities for assessment and observation and plan for them.
Step seven
Identify how the plan will be monitored/evaluated.
It is important to note that everything does not need to be themed, and that a theme need not cover all aspects of learning – in fact, this could be rather overwhelming. Routine activities such as news time or pouring out drinks should still be recognised as learning opportunities although they are not theme related. Free-play and child-initiated activities should not be replaced with themed activities.

Figure 4.13 A theme-planning process

Settings might also plan by selecting some early learning goals or some of the statements from the Development Matters guidance. Some groups might start by choosing calendar events that they want to focus on at key times of the year. There are no right or wrong methods – it's up to settings to develop a system that's effective for them and meets the EYFS framework requirements.

An integrated approach to planning

As you learned in Parts 2 and 3 of this book, it's important to develop an integrated approach to planning. To do this, you must recognise that the activities and experiences you provide for children will generally promote more than one area of their development, since children's learning is not compartmentalised.

By pulling together different areas of learning into activities and experiences when you are planning, you can maximise the potential learning opportunity for children. It's not necessary to mould every activity to fit every area – this would probably make your activity so broad that it would lack purpose – but it is effective to integrate those that are a natural fit.

For example, if you were planning to plant sunflower seeds with the children, you could cover the following:

- Reading about seeds and how they grow, and discussing things already growing in the environment (area of development: communication and language; literacy)

- Handling seeds, looking at them closely (area of development: understanding the world)

- Counting the seeds and sharing them out (area of development: mathematics)

- Planting the seeds gently, thinking about how to care for them (area of development: physical development; understanding the world)

- Pretending to be seeds unfurling and growing to music (area of development: expressive arts and design).

Figure 4.14 Planting sunflower seeds with children promotes a number of areas of learning and development

Taking account of learning styles when planning

People (adults and children) have different preferred styles of learning – that is, ways of learning that are particularly effective for them. The three learning styles are:

- visual
- auditory
- kinaesthetic.

There are differing theories about these, but essentially styles of learning are about the way people:

- **perceive information** – the way they learn information
- **process information** – the way they think and interpret
- **organise and present information** – how they retain and pass on information.

People generally employ all of their senses to perceive, process, organise and present information, but they tend to employ one of the senses more than the others.

Visual learners

Visual learners prefer to learn by seeing. They may:

- prefer an orderly environment
- become distracted by untidiness or movement
- be good at imagining
- be good at reading (they may have good early literacy skills, such as letter recognition)
- particularly enjoy looking at pictures.

Auditory learners

Auditory learners prefer to learn by hearing. They may:

- learn things well through discussion
- think things through when asked questions
- enjoy listening to stories
- like reciting information
- be good at remembering what they are told.

Kinaesthetic learners

Kinaesthetic learners learn through doing, movement and action. They may:

- learn well when they are moving around
- learn best when they have the opportunity to do a task rather than listen to theory
- be good at constructing things
- use expressive movements
- become distracted by activities around them
- prefer to jump right in rather than being shown what to do
- prefer action stories.

When you are planning, you should take into consideration the different learning styles so that you provide a balance of activities that are likely to be beneficial for *all* the children. You should remember, however, that young children are only just establishing their styles, and be wary of labelling them a sole type of learner. Even if you recognise yourself as a particular type of learner, you probably have several traits that fit into the other styles.

Starting points – what do children already know and understand?

When establishing group plans, you need to consider the starting point of all the children – what do they already know and understand? What do they have experience of? This enables you to pitch the activity at the right level.

The starting points will differ within any group of children, even those of the same age, so this requires knowledge of the children and some careful thinking. Consider the best way to group children for activities, and what the role of adults will be in terms of supporting children's learning.

Figure 4.15 Consider the best way to group children for activities

Ask Miranda!

Q: What might an activity that operates on more than one level look like?

A: Here's an example. Practitioner Lisa is planning some tabletop games for her group. She decides to split the group into three subgroups for the activity:

- One group of mainly 4-year-olds will play sound lotto – a game that involves matching pictures on a playing board to the sounds heard on a recording. An adult will be on hand, but the children will be encouraged to manage the game themselves, and to operate the tape recorder.

- A group of mainly 3-year-olds will play sequencing lotto (a game that involves putting pictures into the correct order – for instance, someone posts a letter then the postman delivers the letter). An adult will work with the group, encouraging them to talk about what is happening in the pictures, and the order they should go in.

- A third group, made up mainly of 2½-year-olds, will play picture lotto (a game that involves matching pictures on a playing board to pictures held up on cards) with two adults. They will focus on sharing out the cards, taking turns, naming the pictures and matching.

Using different sources to inform plans

As we've discussed, your own written assessment of children's learning and development is a key source that informs future plans. But when planning activities for an individual child or group of children, it is good practice to use a range of additional sources, as shown in the table on the next page.

Additional sources for planning activities	Importance and benefits
Observations in the form of the mental notes you've made when working with children	• Children may well have progressed since you last made a written assessment.
Children's interests and preferences	• Children need to find activities and opportunities both challenging and enjoyable. • Taking note of children's interests and preferences will help you to meet the statutory requirement to provide children with enjoyment. • It's important to consider where and how children like to play, the resources or toys that they like to play with, or topics or ideas they are interested in. A balanced approach to this is key, as children also need access to new opportunities and experiences. • It's also important to consult children when supporting their learning, to help you to plan activities that are appropriate to their abilities and meet their needs, and to enable you to work with them in ways that suit them best. • Babies and very young children won't be able to tell you what they want verbally. But by being a responsive carer, you can deduce what they want and how they want to do things. Think of it as a kind of 'silent consultation'.

Parents and carers	• The EYFS framework emphasises the importance of working in partnership with parents and carers.
	
	• Familiarity with the setting's plans can help parents and carers to understand how the EYFS framework works and how their children are learning.
	
	• Parents and carers are well placed to provide helpful information which will inform planning, such as:
	
	  – details of interests and preferences outside the setting (perhaps the child is fascinated by people's pets)
	
	  – learning opportunities and experiences that children engage in outside the setting (such as going to family fitness sessions)
	
	  – the progress they have observed their children making.

Additional sources for planning activities	Importance and benefits

	• You may have parents and carers who would like to join in and suggest ideas, which is to be encouraged, or they may be willing to participate in other ways. For instance:
	
	  – collecting resources (such as yoghurt pots to plant seeds in)
	
	  – volunteering practical help during a session.

Colleagues	• Although the key person will take the lead in the observation and assessment of their key children, in group settings no one works in isolation. It is good practice for other practitioners to periodically conduct observations – which will inform planning.
	
	• Planning or consulting with colleagues when planning:
	
	  – allows for a melting pot of ideas
	
	  – shares the workload
	
	  – is an effective way to make sure that everyone understands their roles and responsibilities during a session (including volunteer helpers and students) so that children can be supported effectively, and activities led as intended.
	
	• If a child has special educational needs, the setting's Special Educational Needs Coordinator (SENCO) will also be an important source of input.

Other professionals	• In consultation with parents and carers, specialist support and advice on planning for individual children can be sought from various professionals, such as physiotherapists, psychologists, speech and language therapists. • The setting's SENCO will usually take the lead in arranging this support.

The diagram on the next page shows some of the professionals who may be involved in planning to meet a child's needs. (The support available from professionals can vary between regions in the UK.)

Figure 4.16 Professionals who may be involved in planning to meet a child's needs

Children's participation and involvement in planning

As practitioners, it is up to us to encourage children's participation and involvement in planning their own learning and development activities. It is a statutory requirement of the EYFS framework that settings include child-initiated activities and experiences alongside those initiated by adults. There are several ways of achieving this:

- **Making sure that children have the opportunity to select their own toys and resources:** Settings will have far more resources and equipment than it is practical to make available during a session, so even at 'free play' times, adults influence children's selection by setting out certain resources, usually on a rota system. Ways to overcome this include:

- letting children know that they can choose from the 'put away' toys too. To facilitate this, many settings make sure that resources are accessible to children

- labelling the boxes with pictures of the equipment inside to assist children in making independent selections

- scheduling 'off rota' times when children can select all the activities entirely for themselves

- routinely leaving one area of the setting free for children to set up themselves at every free play session.

- **Noticing children's reactions to the opportunities already available to them, and talking about what they'd like to do in the future:** This links with taking children's interests into account.

  - For instance, if some theme work really engages children, you may decide to spend longer on it, perhaps repeating activities that were originally intended to be one-offs.

  - Older children will be able to answer your questions about future activities; younger children need you to be entirely perceptive.

- **Providing choice whenever possible:** Choice can be offered frequently throughout activities, including those which are adult-initiated. For instance:

  - if children are making Christmas cards, they can choose the colour of their card and which craft materials to use as decoration. They can also decide who their card will be for, what colour pen they would like for the writing inside etc.

  - children may take it in turns to make decisions in group settings when choosing a song at music time, or a book at story time

  - the layout of some settings gives children the freedom to move between the indoor and outdoor play areas at will during free play time.

Adapting your plans to facilitate a child's participation

It's good practice to note on your plans any special support, adaptation, resources or equipment that may be required to facilitate a child's participation. You must make the necessary arrangements as part of your preparation. Where children have individual education plans (IEPs) or play plans, you should incorporate the goals contained within them into the overall planning, indicating them on your plan. For instance:

- a child who lacks confidence when speaking within the group may be identified within the plan as in need of support during circle time, when they may feel under pressure

- you may make a note to enlarge a photograph you want to share with the group, to meet the needs of a child with a visual impairment.

Communicating plans

Once your planning is complete, you must communicate your plans to all relevant people within the setting. Make sure you discuss the roles and responsibilities of other adults – the plan cannot be implemented well if people are unsure what is required of them. Some settings display a copy of the plan in a communal area for all to see, while others distribute a copy of plans to those concerned – this is handy for practitioners to refer to when they may be bringing in resources from home or perhaps working from home during non-contact time. However, it is still advisable to verbally check that everyone has looked at, and is happy with, the plan and their role within it.

> ### ❗ Don't forget
> ---
>
> It is important to remember that plans should be regarded as guidance. They should be a work-in-progress. Be prepared to adapt them when appropriate – some practitioners find this difficult to accept after they have spent time on the planning stage. It is necessary, however, to remain flexible so that your plan fits changing circumstances, meets the needs of the children and makes the most of opportunities that arise unexpectedly.

Underpinning children's future learning

When you're planning, remember that what children learn during their early years underpins all their future learning. Children should be encouraged to develop positive attitudes and dispositions towards their learning. They should *enjoy* their learning so that they become *motivated* to learn. Activities should be playful, and learning and achievements celebrated. If children come to dislike learning at an early age, they may well be unhappy in school – and there are many school years ahead of young children.

Young children often become disillusioned with activities if they are too formal, because they have not yet reached the stage of development when formal teaching experiences are appropriate. Worksheets, for example, are now widely regarded as inappropriate for children in the early years. Children become frustrated by activities that are inappropriate for them in terms of their age, needs or abilities. In addition, they certainly will not learn effectively. Also remember that play is an appropriate vehicle for children's learning because:

- children enjoy playing
- children are intrinsically motivated to play (they are internally driven)
- children can make their own discoveries through play
- children can initiate their own activities and explore their own thoughts and ideas through play
- children can actively learn through play – the learning is a vivid experience
- play is necessary for children's well-being (under the UN Convention on the Rights of the Child, children have a right to play).

EYFS progress check at age 2

The revised EYFS framework now requires practitioners to complete a statutory progress check for every child between the ages of 2 and 3. It's up to settings to agree with parents/carers when it will be most helpful to complete the check for each individual child within this timeframe. However, the EYFS states that, 'It should be provided in time to inform the Healthy Child Programme health and development review at age 2 whenever possible (when health visitors gather information on a child's health and development, allowing them to identify any developmental delay and any particular support from which they think the child/family might benefit).'

This dovetails with the key reason the progress check has been introduced – to enable earlier identification of development needs so that any additional support needed can be put into place as early as possible. Permission to share the progress check with outside professionals (including health visitors) must be given by children's parents or carers.

Non-statutory guidance – *A Know How Guide* – has been produced by the National Children's Bureau to support practitioners in implementing the progress check.

> **❗ Don't forget**
> -
> To access the full *A Know How Guide*, free of charge, go to www.foundationyears.org.uk and enter 'A Know How Guide' into the search box.

What should be covered in the progress check?

The EYFS framework tells us:

- Parents and carers must be provided with a short written summary of their child's development in the prime areas of learning and development (communication and language; personal and social development; physical development).

- The progress check must highlight areas in which a child is progressing well, identifying the child's strengths.

- The progress check must identify any areas where the child's progress is less than expected and in which some additional support might be needed. It must describe the activities and strategies the provider intends to adopt to address any issues or concerns.

- The report must focus particularly on any areas where there is a concern that a child may have a developmental delay (which may indicate a special educational need or disability). In this case, practitioners should develop a targeted plan to support the child's future learning and development, involving other professionals such as the setting's Special Educational Needs Coordinator (SENCO), as appropriate.

Ask Miranda!

Q: Does the progress check have to report on children's progress in the specific areas of learning?

A: No. The EYFS framework states that, beyond coverage of the prime areas, settings can decide for themselves what else the written summary should include. This allows practitioners to reflect the developmental level and needs of the individual child. This is important because, although there isn't an expectation for 2-year-olds to necessarily be progressing beyond the prime areas of learning, some 2-year-olds may already be making some progress in the specific areas of learning and you may wish to comment on this. This is more likely the later the progress check is completed (bearing in mind that the check can be completed at any time between the ages of 2 and 3 years).

❗ Don't forget

The EYFS framework states that if a child moves settings between the ages of 2 and 3, it is expected that the progress check would usually be undertaken by the setting where the child has spent most time.

Obtaining the information that informs the written summary

The written summary will be drawn from the information practitioners have gathered about a child's learning and development through their ongoing observations and assessments (part of every setting's usual practice – see pages 118–217). It's important that a child's progress check is carried out by a practitioner who works directly with them and knows them well – in most cases the child's key worker. However, the views of parents or carers and other professionals who also know the child well should be sought and taken account of in the summary. (This includes both your colleagues and any outside professionals, such as a speech and language therapist. Parental permission is needed to contact outside professionals.) You can read more about this in the *A Know How Guide*.

A Know How Guide reminds us that the non-statutory Development Matters guidance can be used by practitioners to:

- inform and support assessment judgements on a child's development in the prime areas

- identify if there are any areas in which a child may be developing at a faster or slower pace that the expected level of progress for their age

- inform and support their discussions with parents (see below) and other professionals, where relevant.

❗ Don't forget

- -

You can download the Development Matters guidance free of charge at www.foundationyears.org.uk.

Ask Miranda!

Q: Are practitioners only supposed to share written information with parents and carers at the 2-year-old check and towards the end of the EYFS when the EYFS profile is completed?

A: These are the statutory times when particular, specified information must be recorded and shared with parents and carers. However, practitioners will be carrying out observations and assessments from the time children begin attending their setting. It's good practice to regularly share findings with parents and carers, and to agree any support necessary for the child. This is generally achieved through periodic meetings between the key worker and parent/carer, in which written assessment documents are shared and discussed. When and how interim written summaries are produced (outside the check at age 2 and the EYFS profile) will be down to the policies and procedures of your individual setting. Remember, though, that the EYFS requirement for parents and carers to be 'kept up to date with their child's progress and development' must be met.

❗ Don't forget

- -

A *Know How Guide* reminds us that the written summary should be based on the skills, knowledge, understanding and behaviour that the child demonstrates consistently and independently.

Format of the progress check

Unlike the EYFS profile, which is completed towards the end of the EYFS (see page 240), there are no set forms to complete for the progress check at age 2. Settings are able to devise their own way of recording the written summary, giving them the freedom to choose the method that will dovetail best with the usual style of the observations/assessments/reports produced by the individual setting. Three excellent yet very different examples of how settings organise their reports are included on pages 23–33 of *A Know How Guide* – it will be helpful to take a look and spend some time considering how they compare and contrast. Ultimately you should follow the method of recording adopted by your own setting.

Use of the information within the 2-year-old check

The 2-year-old check is an opportunity for practitioners to focus on and further understand the needs of the 2-year-old child they are working with, as a clear picture of their development emerges. Practitioners should use this information to inform their ongoing planning at the setting by devising activities and experiences for the child which:

- meet any individual needs that may have been identified

- support and extend development.

The information is also used to inform others about the child's development within the prime areas of learning. This includes:

- parents and carers (see page 239)

- colleagues within the setting

- outside professionals where relevant, including health visitors.

> **❗ Don't forget**
>
> The EYFS framework states that, 'Taking account of information from the progress check (which reflects ongoing, regular observation of children's development) should help ensure that health visitors can identify children's needs accurately and fully at the health review'.

Working in partnership with parents and carers to support development

The EYFS framework tells us that, in addition to providing parents and carers with the information already mentioned in this section (see the bullet points under 'What should be covered in the progress check?' on page 235), practitioners must discuss with parents and carers how the summary of development can be used to support the child's learning at home. To achieve this, practitioners should ensure that they:

- give parents and carers a clear picture of the child's development

- help parents and carers to understand the child's learning and development needs, and the types of activity that will promote them

- explain the activities that are planned or already used to support the child's development within the setting, and the activities or strategies that can be used at home. A discussion about the activities or strategies that are already used at home will inform this.

Examples of activities or strategies discussed for use at home by parents could include:

- spending some time each day sharing a book together

- encouraging the child to carry out some self-care tasks with more independence, such as supporting them to turn the taps on and off themselves when washing their hands

- using the 'running commentary' style of communication when doing things around the home, to ensure there is frequent interaction between the child and adult even when parents are busy doing chores

- sharing rhymes or songs used within the setting at home, going at the child's own pace.

See *A Know How Guide* for further information.

EYFS profile 2012

The EYFS framework requires that all children are assessed in the summer term of their reception year. This assessment is called the EYFS profile. It focuses on a child's overall attainment of the early learning goals as they reach the end of the Early Years Foundation Stage.

In autumn 2012, the Standards and Testing Agency (STA), an executive agency of the Department for Education, will publish the *EYFS Profile Handbook*. The handbook is designed to support teachers and other professionals to undertake EYFS profile assessments. The handbook will be supported by exemplification material (examples), to help teachers and other professionals make accurate judgements about each child's level of attainment.

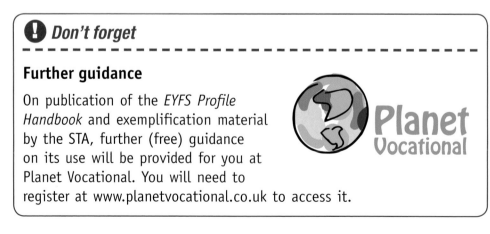

Sharing assessments with parents, carers, colleagues and outside professionals

Practitioners must share the findings of their assessments with parents and carers on a regular basis. This is in addition to sharing the findings of the statutory progress check at age 2 and the EYFS profile.

Informing parents and carers about their child's progress is a crucial part of working in partnership. Many settings do this effectively by arranging a time for parents and carers to meet privately with their child's key worker. At the meeting, the key worker talks about the assessment methods that have been used and the outcome of the assessment. They summarise the progress that has been made and establish what the child is expected to learn next, drawing attention to any areas that may need particular attention. Parents and carers are often keen to know how they can support their child's learning at home, so practitioners are advised to think this through before the meeting. If a child has not been progressing as expected, this will need to be discussed. The matter should be handled openly but sensitively. The practitioner should ensure that they also focus on what the child *can* do and the achievements they *have* made, as this will give parents and carers a balanced report. Practitioners will want to work in partnership with parents and carers with regard to what should happen next, and to decide if outside support is needed.

Figure 4.17 Assessments should be shared with parents and carers

Practitioners should also share their assessment findings with appropriate colleagues and outside professionals (with the permission of the parents/ carers).

Sharing assessment findings with all these parties ensures that everyone working with a particular group of children understands how each child is progressing, what each child is expected to learn next, and how this will be achieved. This informs practitioners' practical work with children – they know how to support them effectively to encourage and extend their learning and developmental progress.

> **❶ Don't forget**
> -
> The EYFS framework says that, 'Parents and/or carers should be kept up to date with their child's progress and development. Practitioners should address any learning and development needs in partnership with parents and/or carers, and any relevant professionals'.

5 Ofsted and the safeguarding and welfare requirements

The safeguarding and welfare requirements

The EYFS framework sets out the safeguarding and welfare requirements which early years providers have a legal requirement to meet. They explain what providers must do to:

- safeguard children
- ensure the suitability of adults who have contact with children
- promote good health
- manage behaviour
- maintain records, policies and procedures.

The introduction to the safeguarding and welfare requirements within the EYFS framework tells us that children learn best when:

- they are healthy, safe and secure
- their individual needs are met
- they have positive relationships with the adults caring for them.

> **❗ Don't forget**
>
> The safeguarding and welfare requirements set out just the *minimum* standards that providers must meet. They are not benchmarks for best practice, and high quality providers will often exceed the minimum standards. For example, a day nursery may exceed the minimum staff:child ratio.

It is good practice for all practitioners to know and understand the safeguarding and welfare requirements, which form Section 3 of the Statutory Framework for the Early Years Foundation Stage.

To download, go to www.foundationyears.org.uk and click on 'EYFS 2012'. You will benefit from reading them in full in conjunction with this part of the book, which takes each section of the requirements in turn and gives examples of how they impact on everyday practice in early years settings. You were first introduced to the safeguarding and welfare requirements on page 28.

Figure 5.1 Children learn best when they have positive relationships with the adults caring for them

Child protection

EYFS link

It is important that you know and understand the safeguarding and welfare requirements relating to child protection. Make sure you read sections 3.4–3.8 on pages 13–14 of the EYFS framework.

Examples of impact on everyday practice

The use of mobile phones and cameras in early years settings

Coverage of the use of mobile phones and cameras in settings (requirement 3.4) was introduced following the prosecution in 2009 of a practitioner in a Plymouth day nursery. She had used her mobile phone to take, and then share, inappropriate photographs of children in her care.

Ofsted acknowledges that mobile phones do have a place in early years settings – especially as not all settings have easy access to a landline – so they are not banned. (It is actually a requirement for providers to take a mobile phone with them when on an outing.) Make sure that you understand your setting's guidelines for using and storing both your own mobile and any phones that belong to the setting.

> **❗ Don't forget**
> -
> It's a good idea to read Ofsted's information sheet on mobile phones. To download, go to www.ofsted.gov.uk, click on 'Resources', then 'Mobile phones' and follow the links.
>
> The Department for Education has also published guidance on the use of mobile phones, which you can download at www.education.gov.uk.

> **❗ Don't forget**
> -
> You must have written parental permission to take photos of children. Photos must only be taken and used for the purposes explained in the permission guidance. Always follow your own setting's policies and procedures.

Safeguarding children

You are required not only to undertake training on safeguarding policies and procedures but also to have up-to-date knowledge of safeguarding issues. It's up to your employer to provide this so make sure that you ask for training if it has not been offered to you. The member of staff designated as the 'lead practitioner for safeguarding' will normally be your first contact. Regularly reading industry publications (such as *Nursery World)* and signing up for newsletters on industry websites (such as www.foundationyears.org.uk) will help you to stay up to date with legislation and best practice.

'Working Together to Safeguard Children' is a document which sets out how organisations and individuals should work together to safeguard and promote the welfare of children and young people in accordance with the Children Act 1989 and the Children Act 2004. Part 1 of the document is issued as statutory guidance, which means that providers and other agencies must comply, by law. Your setting's policies and procedures will take account of this guidance and state how your setting will meet its responsibilities in practice. 'Working Together to Safeguard Children' is aimed at practitioners and frontline managers who work directly with children, so you should download and read the document for yourself.

Figure 5.2 Safeguarding policies and procedures must cover the use of mobile phones and cameras

> **! Don't forget**
>
> -
>
> To download a copy of 'Working Together to Safeguard Children', go to www.education.gov.uk, click on 'Publications' and follow the links.

Suitable people

EYFS link

It is important that you know and understand the safeguarding and welfare requirements relating to suitable people. Make sure you read sections 3.9–3.13 on pages 14–15 of the EYFS framework.

Examples of impact on everyday practice

Not allowing practitioners to have unsupervised contact with children before checks have been completed

It's fairly common for new staff to begin working at a setting before checks on their suitability to work with children have been completed (including through a criminal records check). This is because the checking procedures can take some time. If you find yourself in this position, it's essential that you comply with requirement 3.11 – not to have unsupervised contact with children being cared for – until your checks are finalised. Settings are generally very good at ensuring this requirement is met, but there is room for error. Consider the following example.

A new member of staff who has not yet been checked is employed in a nursery baby room alongside two colleagues, who work together to ensure she is not left unsupervised with the children. One of her colleagues says she's leaving the room to change a child's nappy. The other colleague is busy sharing a song with one of the babies and doesn't hear this. After a few moments, he says he is leaving the room to fetch the milk that one of his key children is due to have shortly.

If you had been the new member of staff in this case, you could have prevented the requirements from being breached by informing the second colleague that they needed to hang on for a moment until the first practitioner returned. Alternatively, you could have offered to fetch the milk for them, and explained the reason why.

Disqualification (all registered providers)

EYFS link

It is important that you know and understand the safeguarding and welfare requirements relating to disqualification (all registered providers). Make sure you read sections 3.14–3.16 on pages 15–16 of the EYFS framework.

Examples of impact on everyday practice

Disclosure of information which may affect your suitability to work with children

It's your responsibility to be entirely honest in disclosing any convictions, cautions, court orders, reprimands and warnings which may affect your suitability to work with children. It is the law. This applies throughout the time you work at a setting, not just at the time of the initial suitability checks.

Staff taking medication/other substances

EYFS link

It is important that you know and understand the safeguarding and welfare requirements relating to staff taking medication/other substances. Make sure you read section 3.17 on page 16 of the EYFS framework.

Examples of impact on everyday practice

Alcohol

You must never be under the influence of alcohol or any other substance which may affect your ability to care for children. This includes still being under the influence of alcohol or any other substance taken the day or evening before a shift at work.

Medication

If you begin taking medication which may affect your ability to care for children, you must discuss this with your employer without delay. For example, you should discuss medication which may affect alertness or your mood or have side effects that make you feel unwell.

Make sure you are clear on the procedures for storing your own medication as this may differ to the procedures for storing children's medication. This will be of particular note if you usually keep emergency medication – such as an asthma inhaler – with you on your person.

Figure 5.3 Tell your employer if you begin taking medication which may affect your ability to care for children

Staff qualifications, training, support and skills

EYFS link

It is important that you know and understand the safeguarding and welfare requirements relating to staff qualifications, training, support and skills. Make sure you read sections 3.18–3.25 on pages 17–18 of the EYFS framework.

Examples of impact on everyday practice

Getting the most out of training opportunities

While the wording of the requirements emphasises the employer's role in providing its practitioners with appropriate ongoing training opportunities, it's true to say that how much you get out of learning opportunities relates to how much you put into them. Make the most of valuable training opportunities, such as courses, seminars or in-house training, by:

- giving your best attention
- contributing where possible
- completing any necessary exercises, such as background reading
- committing sufficient time to other tasks, such as assignments or projects.

Staff appraisals

The same applies to job appraisals – it pays to prepare well and think about your strengths, weaknesses and any training you would like to access ahead of the appraisal.

❗ Don't forget

It's unlikely you will stay with one employer throughout your career so it's up to you to take responsibility for your continued professional development.

Key person

EYFS link

It is important that you know and understand the safeguarding and welfare requirements relating to the key person. Make sure you read section 3.26 on page 18 of the EYFS framework.

Figure 5.4 It takes time to build key
relationships with children

Examples of impact on everyday practice

The role of the key worker

Building key relationships with children and their families requires
time and trust. As you learned on page 37, an important part of a
key worker's role is to take account of their key children's needs when
planning activities and experiences. This applies both on a one-to-one
basis and when children take part in a group. It's important for
you to understand the approach your setting takes to ensuring key
responsibilities are met within the everyday schedule.

Staff:child ratios

EYFS link

It is important that you know and understand the safeguarding and welfare requirements relating to staff:child ratios. Make sure you read sections 3.27–3.38 on pages 18–21 of the EYFS framework.

Ask Miranda!

Q: Do I need to know all the different staff:child ratios as I am finding them confusing?

A: The staff:child ratios outlined on these pages may well seem rather complicated to you, as they differ according to circumstances – such as the type of setting and the level of qualifications held by staff. But you only need to understand the ratios for the type of setting and the circumstances in which you currently work. If you are unsure, ask a senior colleague to explain which of the staff:child ratio requirements apply to your setting and why. (There are several footnotes in this section of the full version of the safeguarding and welfare requirements.)

Figure 5.5 The correct staff:child ratio must be maintained to ensure children's safety and well-being

Examples of settings meeting the ratio requirements

The following examples show how the staff:child ratio requirements may work in practice.

Children aged under 2

In one nursery baby room caring for 12 under-2s, there are four members of staff. Two are qualified to level 3, one to level 2 and one is currently unqualified. There is also a 16-year-old trainee who is not counted in the ratio.

Children aged 2

In one children's centre, the toddler room cares for 12 2-year-olds. There are three members of staff working in this room. Two are qualified to level 3, and one is currently unqualified.

Children aged 3 and over in early years provision

In one pre-school caring for 24 children aged 3 to 5 years, there are three members of staff. One member of staff is qualified to level 3, one is qualified to level 2 and one is currently unqualified. There is also a 16-year-old trainee who is not counted in the ratio.

Children aged 3 and over in a maintained school

In one nursery class in a maintained school caring for 24 children aged 3 to 5 years, there are two members of staff. One member of staff is a qualified teacher and one is qualified to level 3.

Staff:child ratios – childminders

EYFS link

It is important that you know and understand the safeguarding and welfare requirements relating to childminders. Make sure you read sections 3.39–3.41 on page 21 of the EYFS framework.

Examples of childminders meeting the ratio requirements

The following examples show how the requirements may work in practice:

- One childminder cares for one 8-month-old baby, one 18-month-old child and one 22-month-old child from 8am to 6pm.

- One childminder cares for six children aged 5 to 8 years before and after school. Some of the children also attend during school holidays.

- One childminder cares for her own 9-month-old baby full time. On Mondays and Tuesdays she also cares for two children aged 3 to 5 years all day, and a 5-year-old before school only. On Wednesdays, Thursdays and Fridays she cares for twin 2-year-old boys.

- One childminder is about to start working with an assistant. Between them they plan to care for up to six young children on a full-time basis. No more than two of these children will be under 1 year old.

> **! Don't forget**
> --
> If you are a childminder or a nanny you will find support and advice online at www.ncma.org.uk.

Health – medicines

EYFS link

It is important that you know and understand the safeguarding and welfare requirements relating to medicines. Make sure you read sections 3.42–3.44 on pages 21–22 of the EYFS framework.

Examples of impact on everyday practice

Administering medicines

If a child in your care may need to be administered medicine that requires medical or technical knowledge, you will need additional training under requirement 3.43. For instance, you may be trained by a nurse or health visitor on how to give a potentially lifesaving injection to a child who has a severe food allergy.

You must ensure that you understand and follow your setting's procedures for administering all medication. For instance, you may be required to always administer medicine in partnership with a colleague. This approach can be used to build in an extra level of vigilance – two people are required to agree that the correct medication has been selected and the correct dose measured before it is administered, and both check and sign the medication log afterwards.

Health – food and drink

EYFS link

It is important that you know and understand the safeguarding and welfare requirements relating to food and drink. Make sure you read sections 3.45–3.47 on page 22 of the EYFS framework.

Examples of impact on everyday practice

Food hygiene

Settings will usually have extensive procedures to ensure that food and drink is stored and handled safely, and to ensure that children's dietary requirements are met. Although only a requirement in group settings, it is best practice (in complying with requirement 3.46) for all practitioners to acquire a basic food hygiene certificate. This involves undertaking a short food hygiene course and multiple-choice exam.

The provision of drinking water

Your setting may use strategies to encourage children to drink water outside snack and meal times (because of the health and well-being benefits, including increased levels of concentration).

Figure 5.6 Drinking water must be available at all times

For example, adults may be asked to act as role models by taking regular drinks of water themselves throughout sessions – 'I think I'll have a quick drink of water before we start our story ...'

Health – accident or injury

EYFS link

It is important that you know and understand the safeguarding and welfare requirements relating to accident or injury. Make sure you read sections 3.48–3.49 on pages 22–23 of the EYFS framework.

Examples of impact on everyday practice

First aid training

It's good practice for all practitioners to undertake first aid training. (This does not necessarily mean you will be the appointed first aider for your setting.) First aid certificates must be renewed every three years. Make it a priority to receive first aid training and keep this up throughout your career. It is a useful life skill whether or not it is required in the workplace.

❗ Don't forget

It's worth all settings considering that they may have a serious problem if there's only one first aider present and that person becomes injured or ill themselves. It is best practice to have more than one first aider present at all sessions.

Managing behaviour

EYFS link

It is important that you know and understand the safeguarding and welfare requirements relating to managing behaviour. Make sure you read sections 3.50–3.51 on page 23 of the EYFS framework.

Q: What is meant by 'physical intervention was taken for the purposes of averting immediate danger of personal injury ...' in requirement 3.51?

A: 'Physical intervention' is where practitioners use reasonable force to prevent children from injuring themselves or others or damaging property.

Examples of impact on everyday practice

Behaviour management policies and procedures

Not only is it crucial in terms of requirement 3.50 that you understand and follow your setting's behaviour management policies, it is also essential for children's well-being. Promoting positive behaviour and managing inappropriate behaviour effectively in group settings requires practitioners to have a consistent approach. This ensures fairness and stability. Settings can approach rules, boundaries and sanctions in different ways, so it's important for all staff to be fully inducted. Most settings will set aside regular time in staff meetings to discuss ongoing behaviour management.

You can consult the named practitioner responsible for behaviour management within your setting for support and advice at any time. They may also provide in-house training for staff if requested.

Safety and suitability of premises, environment and equipment

EYFS link

It is important that you know and understand the safeguarding and welfare requirements relating to the safety and suitability of premises, the environment and equipment. Make sure you read the following sections of the EYFS framework:

- Safety – 3.53–3.54, pages 23–24

- Smoking – 3.55, page 24

- Premises – 3.56–3.62, pages 24–25
- Risk assessment – 3.63, page 25
- Outings – 3.64–3.65, pages 25–26.

Figure 5.7 Provision must be made for children who wish to sleep

Examples of impact on everyday practice

Health and safety policies and procedures

Remember that the safeguarding and welfare requirements set out the *minimum* standards below which no setting may fall, and that individual settings will often exceed some of the requirements. It is therefore important that you know and understand the health and safety policies and procedures that your own setting has in place. You should have a detailed health and safety induction when starting a new position. In addition to the varying levels of expectation in settings, many health and safety decisions depend on a setting's particular physical environment, the services provided and the needs of the children currently cared for.

Risk assessment requirements

Many settings are now reviewing their risk assessment procedures in response to the revised EYFS framework. The revised requirements clarify that it is for providers to judge whether a risk assessment needs to be recorded in writing. (You will probably receive in-house training from your setting to outline the criteria for completing a written risk assessment.) In the early days of implementing these changes, as people gain confidence with the new requirements, settings may suggest that practitioners buddy up so everyone can discuss a written risk assessment decision with a colleague.

❗ Don't forget

The indoor space requirements within section 3.56 of the safeguarding and welfare requirements is based on the useable areas of rooms occupied by the children and doesn't include storage areas, thoroughfares, dedicated staff areas, cloakrooms, utility rooms, kitchens and toilets.

Equal opportunities

EYFS link

It is important that you know and understand the safeguarding and welfare requirements relating to equal opportunities. Make sure you read section 3.66 on page 26 of the EYFS framework.

Examples of impact on everyday practice

Support for children with special educational needs or disabilities

It's good practice to consider the needs of every child when you are planning activities and experiences both for individual children and for the group as a whole. If activities aren't inclusive, you should make adaptations to overcome barriers to participation. For example, to enable the participation of a child who uses a wheelchair, you may plan for other children to play parachute games kneeling up as opposed to standing up.

Also, consider the support that individual children may require from staff during particular activities or everyday routines, and note this on plans when appropriate. For instance, a child who experiences communication and language difficulties may have one-to-one support assigned to them at circle time.

You should liaise regularly with your setting's Special Educational Needs Coordinator (SENCO), who can offer information, advice and practical support in meeting a child's needs. They will also have details of local training opportunities which could help you to develop your skills in this area.

There is further information in Part 3 of this book on promoting and valuing diversity and difference (including religious and cultural differences). See the sections on 'Personal, social and emotional development' and 'Understanding of the world', which also explore how you can encourage children to value and respect each other.

Information and records

EYFS link

It is important that you know and understand the safeguarding and welfare requirements relating to information and records. Make sure you read sections 3.67–3.70 on pages 26–27 of the EYFS framework.

Examples of impact on everyday practice

Sharing confidential information

Confidential information will be shared on a 'need to know' basis within a setting. This means that you may be aware of information that some of your colleagues do not need to know. For instance, you may be aware of difficulties within the family of your key child. If you are unsure whether to share information, check with your supervisor. Your setting's confidentiality policy is also there to guide you.

Ask Miranda!

Q: Do parents and carers have an automatic right to see any information held about their child?

A: The Data Protection Act 1998 (DPA) gives parents and carers the right to access information about their child held by a provider. However, the DPA also sets out specific exemptions under which certain personal information may, under specific circumstances, be withheld from release. For example, a relevant professional will need to give careful consideration as to whether the disclosure of certain information about a child could cause harm either to the child or any other individual. It is therefore essential that all providers/staff in early years settings have an understanding of how data protection laws operate.

For further guidance on data protection, go to the Information Commissioner's Office website www.ico.gov.uk, click on 'Early years and childcare' and follow the links.

Figure 5.8 Records must be stored securely

Information and records – information about the child

EYFS link

It is important that you know and understand the safeguarding and welfare requirements relating to information about the child. Make sure you read section 3.71 on page 27 of the EYFS framework.

Examples of impact on everyday practice

Storing and updating information about children

These records must be stored securely and confidentially in line with the requirements of the Data Protection Act 1998 (DPA). This applies to both paper-based and electronic records. Amendments must be made to records immediately if information changes, for example, if a parent moves house.

Information and records – Information for parents and carers

EYFS link

It is important that you know and understand the safeguarding and welfare requirements relating to information for parents and carers. Make sure you read section 3.72 on page 27 of the EYFS framework.

Examples of impact on everyday practice

Sharing information with parents and carers

Please refer back to page 37 in Part 2 on the responsibilities of key workers in sharing information with parents and carers.

Information and records – Complaints

EYFS link

It is important that you know and understand the safeguarding and welfare requirements relating to complaints. Make sure you read sections 3.73–3.74 on pages 27–28 of the EYFS framework.

Examples of impact on everyday practice

Procedures for dealing with complaints

You must know and understand the complaints procedure at your setting, as a parent may voice a complaint directly to you and you will need to know how to respond.

You may also find yourself involved in the investigation of a complaint. This could be either:

- directly – a complaint received may implicate you, or it may be your job to investigate if you hold a senior position, or

- indirectly – you may be asked to give an account of an event or events you have witnessed, or to share your thoughts and opinions on a certain topic.

> ### ❗ Don't forget
> --
> It is important to remain professional, to stay calm and follow your setting's procedures when dealing with complaints.

Information and records – Information about the provider

> ### EYFS link
>
> It is important that you know and understand the safeguarding and welfare requirements relating to information about the provider. Make sure you read section 3.75 on page 28 of the EYFS framework.

Examples of impact on everyday practice

Documentation that needs to be held by the setting/employer

You must provide your employer with written details of your address and telephone number.

You also need to comply with your setting's procedures for keeping track of who is present and working on a daily basis. For most practitioners, this involves manually signing in and out of the premises at the start and end of each shift, including at the beginning and end of lunch breaks (although this may depend on whether you leave the premises). Some settings may record this information automatically by means of an entry/exit system, for example, through a personalised swipe card or finger printing.

Changes that must be notified to Ofsted

EYFS link

It is important that you know and understand the safeguarding and welfare requirements relating to changes that must be notified to Ofsted. Make sure you read sections 3.76–3.77 on pages 28–29 of the EYFS framework.

Examples of impact on everyday practice

Notifying your employer of any changes which could affect your suitability to work with children

If you change address, you must make your employer aware of this immediately. The same applies if anything happens that could affect your suitability to work with children, such as receiving a warning from police or taking certain types of medication (see page 248). This information needs to be provided to Ofsted.

Ask Miranda!

Q: Do all early years providers have to have separate written policies to cover the EYFS requirements?

A: Schools are not required to have separate written policies to cover EYFS requirements if the requirements are already met through an existing school policy.

Childminders are not required to have written policies and procedures, but they must be able to explain them to parents, carers and others, including Ofsted inspectors. They must also ensure that any assistants follow these policies and procedures. However, many childminders do record their policies and

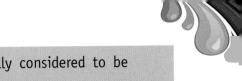

procedures in writing, and this is generally considered to be best practice.

All other early years providers are required to have the necessary policies and procedures recorded in writing.

Ofsted regulation and inspection

Ofsted is the body that regularly inspects all early years settings to judge their quality and standards for the welfare, learning and development of children – as set out in the Statutory Framework for the Early Years Foundation Stage. (Ofsted also inspects childcare providers outside the early years to check that they comply with all the requirements of registration, but does not make any judgements about the quality of their setting.)

Inspectors give each setting one of four grades:

- Outstanding
- Good
- Satisfactory
- Inadequate.

To reach an overall judgement, inspectors will ask themselves 'What is it like for a child here?'

Inspection results are measured in one of three ways, indicating how well the provider is meeting the requirements of registration:

- Met
- Not met – and notice to improve
- Not met – and enforcement measures taken. (Ultimately, Ofsted has the power to close down a setting which does not comply with requirements.)

Ask Miranda!

Q: What is the procedure for an Ofsted inspection?

A: Ofsted doesn't usually give notice of an early years inspection
This is so inspectors can see the setting running normally, but
an inspector may telephone beforehand to check that children
are attending on the day of the inspection or whether a holiday
play scheme is operating. If a setting does receive notice of an
inspection, staff must tell parents that an inspection is due to
take place.

During the inspection, the inspector will observe everyday practice
within the setting, speak with members of staff, assess the
premises and consider documentation – such as plans, assessments
and records held about staff and children.

At the end of an inspection, the inspector will give verbal
feedback on their findings to senior member/s of staff.

Shortly after the inspection, an inspection report will be published
on Ofsted's website, www.ofsted.gov.uk. This is accessible to the
public, and parents are advised to read inspection reports when they
are choosing an early years setting for their child. The setting must
also make the report available to the existing parents and carers.

Preparing for an inspection and the inspection process

Ofsted produces factsheets on what happens before, during and after an
inspection. The factsheets include guidance on preparing for inspection
(such as having the right documentation available). Up-to-date factsheets
are normally available on the Ofsted website.

Revised early years regulation and inspection

In response to the revisions made to the EYFS framework, Ofsted must
revise its own frameworks for the regulation and inspection of early years
providers. Ofsted has consulted parents, carers and early years providers
as part of this process. New guidelines on inspection under the revised
EYFS framework are expected from Ofsted during 2012. At the time of
writing, they are not yet available. See the Don't forget section on page
269 for details about accessing this information when it is released.

Figure 5.9 Ofsted inspectors don't usually give notification of an inspection visit

As a result of the changes to the EYFS framework, Ofsted has reviewed the way in which it:

- registers new applicants who wish to become childcare providers on the Early Years Register, delivering the Early Years Foundation Stage

- inspects providers who are on the register, to ensure that they continue to meet the requirements of the Early Years Foundation Stage

- deals with information which suggests that a registered provider may not be meeting requirements.

> *Regulation of providers on the Early Years Register: A report on the responses to the consultation, Ofsted, May 2012*

Questions asked as part of the consultation

The consultation covered six key issues that will underpin the new Ofsted frameworks. Consultees (including parents, carers, practitioners and providers) were asked about the extent to which they agreed or disagreed with the following:

1. The inspection criteria the inspectors will take into account in making their inspection judgements.

2. Ofsted should ask providers themselves to look into minor matters that do not suggest any risk to children.

Ask Miranda!

Q: What types of matters are considered 'minor matters'?

A: Minor matters are typically complaints that have been brought to the attention of Ofsted, for example, a parent may have complained about a lack of opportunities to play outside in the winter.

3. Ofsted should retain the current notice periods for inspection.

Ask Miranda!

Q: What are 'notice periods for inspection'?

A: These are the amount of notice given to providers before an inspection takes place.

4. Ofsted should continue to make an online self-evaluation document available for providers.

Ask Miranda!

Q: What is the purpose of the online self-evaluation document?

A: This is a document providers can complete to help them to assess their own practice and to prepare for inspection.

5. Ofsted should produce only a short summary report for small-scale providers such as childminders.

Ask Miranda!

Q: Why might small-scale providers only receive a summary report?

A: The consultation looked at whether or not it is necessary for small-scale providers, such as childminders who care for a very few children in a relatively small space, to receive the same detailed inspection report as larger providers, such as nurseries.

Ofsted and the safeguarding and welfare requirements

6. Ofsted should use electronic communications as its main means of communicating with applicants for registration and registered providers.

As of July 2012, the results of the consultation are being used to help Ofsted to develop and implement new frameworks, which will apply from September 2012. Ofsted is aiming to publish the new frameworks and accompanying guidance during the summer of 2012.

❗ *Don't forget*

Further guidance and information

Following the release of the frameworks, further (free) guidance will be provided for you at Planet Vocational. You will need to register at www.planetvocational.co.uk to access it.

Ofsted is expected to make full information about the revised frameworks for regulation and inspection available on its website. Go to www.ofsted.gov.uk, click on 'Early years and childcare' and follow the links.

❗ *Don't forget*

Under the Childcare Act 2006 and its supporting regulations, Ofsted has responsibility for regulating and inspecting providers who are required to register on the Early Years Register. All providers on the Early Years Register must deliver the Early Years Foundation Stage framework.

Ofsted's proposals for the regulation and inspection of early years providers (following consultation)

Since Ofsted's revised frameworks aren't yet available, Ofsted has, in the meantime, published the report on the results of the consultation ('Regulation of providers on the Early Years Register'), which provides an indication of some of the key changes that can be expected in the final revised framework for regulation and inspection. At the end of the report, Ofsted indicates that there will also be some further changes that were not part of the consultation questions but which they intend to implement from September 2012. So, whilst the report on the results of the consultation gives an indication of some of the likely changes, it's important to understand that it does not give a complete overview of all the changes ahead.

Below are the key findings and proposals (published in the report on the responses to consultation) that have emerged from the questions asked.

1 Asking providers to look into minor concerns

There was strong support for this suggestion. Respondents commented, however, that they want to be clearer about what Ofsted considers to be a minor concern. Ofsted will therefore:

- offer further guidance to providers and parents on what they mean by a 'minor concern that a provider will be asked to look into', including examples

- set out for providers expectations on recording and sharing their information about such concerns with inspectors at inspection

- provide clearer information about how they will deal with concerns raised with them by parents.

2 Inspection notice periods

The responses to this question were positive. Ofsted therefore believes it is right to retain the current notice periods.

3 Online self-evaluation form

As respondents were keen for Ofsted to retain the online self-evaluation form with some changes. They will review and revise it to make it shorter and less repetitive.

4 Summary inspection reports for small-scale providers

The majority of respondents supported this suggestion. From the comments made during the consultation, it is clear that parents in particular would value a short summary at the beginning of every inspection report, but that fuller information should be available where this is relevant. Every report will therefore carry a short summary about the provider's main strengths and weaknesses, but additional material

Figure 5.10 In response to consultation, the online self-evaluation form will be kept, with some changes

will be available for all reports; the amount of additional material will be based on the size and organisation of the setting and not on the type of provider.

5 Inspection criteria

Respondents supported the criteria but felt that, if possible, they could be made simpler. Ofsted will therefore review the inspection criteria to see if they can make them simpler and shorter, to deal with concerns about the number of aspects an inspector needs to cover during the inspection. In reviewing the criteria, they will ensure that they don't lose any significant information that underpins key judgements made.

Respondents welcomed the move towards greater use of electronic communications but wanted to ensure that those without access to a computer would not be disadvantaged. Ofsted will therefore move towards the use of electronic communication as the default position for communicating with applicants (applying to become providers) and providers in future.

Other matters

When Ofsted publishes its guidance on inspection under the revised EYFS framework, they will outline any other proposals (that haven't come from the consultation questions) which they intend to implement from September 2012.

Coping with inspection

Practitioners often find that the best way to feel more confident about inspection is to be well prepared. It makes sense, therefore, to follow the guidance given below.

There's no doubt that many practitioners experience some stress when an Ofsted inspector arrives. It's perfectly normal to feel a bit anxious when someone is judging the quality of your work and setting, just as it's normal to feel nervous when having a job interview or an annual work appraisal.

If you are a dedicated practitioner, however, fulfilling your duties to a professional standard, there's no need to worry unduly. And, generally speaking, the more inspections you undergo, the less stressful they become.

Identifying your concerns

If you do feel more than a little general anxiety about the prospect of inspection, it's worth spending some time trying to pinpoint why.

Ask yourself exactly what it is you're worried about and make a list of your areas of concern. Next, be absolutely honest about the reason behind each concern. For instance:

1. A practitioner may be worried that an inspector will ask her about the setting's procedures for supporting a child whose development is found to be delayed at the 2-year-old check. This could be based on an underlying concern that the practitioner hasn't personally had

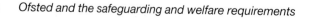

to action the procedures and so she would be trying to remember the setting's guidance rather than talking from experience. She's not sure she is familiar enough with the guidance to do this.

2. A practitioner may be worried that an inspector will find fault with his planning documents. This could be based on an underlying concern that he may not promote the early learning goals for a certain area of learning as well as he might, perhaps due to a lack of training in this area.

3. A practitioner may be worried that an inspector will find fault with the way assessment is carried out at her setting. This could be based on an underlying concern about whether she is doing too much or too little paperwork in the light of the new requirement that assessment paperwork 'should not be excessive'.

Dealing with your concerns

Once you've identified your underlying concerns, think about what you can do to minimise them, then take appropriate action.

1. In the first scenario above, the practitioner could ask the setting's Special Educational Needs Coordinator (SENCO) to meet with her and discuss the setting's procedures on supporting a child who's been found to have a delay in an aspect of their development at the 2-year-old check. The SENCO is likely to be able to tell her about the steps that were taken to support and child and their family in a real situation, which will help the practitioner to better understand how the procedures work in practice.

2. In the second scenario, the practitioner could speak to his supervisor and explain that he'd like to access training on the particular area of learning causing him concern. In the meantime, he may read more about the area, and perhaps ask a colleague to buddy up with him on his planning.

3. In the third scenario, the practitioner needs to raise her concern about the way the setting approaches assessment, as this is a procedural issue that affects the way that everyone works. It would probably be most appropriate to do this in a team meeting (although this does depend on the setting – it may be protocol to raise the concern with a supervisor first). The issue can then be discussed and, if necessary, additional guidance/information can be sought (for example, advice from an advisory teacher, or a member

of staff might attend a seminar on assessment and cascade the information to colleagues). As the assessment procedures are new, it may be appropriate to monitor them for a time to see how effective they are, or it may become apparent that some changes should be made straight away.

As you can see from the three examples, acknowledging and addressing concerns can impact on your continued professional development. It's also a lot better than holding onto a nagging doubt or worry.

During the inspection

During the inspection, concentrate on the task in hand. Remember to focus on the children and what you should be doing for them, just as you normally would. *Don't* show more interest in what the inspector is watching or who he or she is talking to!

> ### ❗ Don't forget
> --
> Remember that your colleagues and employers are there to support you in your role, so do talk to them if you feel overwhelmed about any aspect of inspection.

Settings generally have a short meeting to debrief straight after an inspection. It's important to give colleagues this time to talk about their shared experience and to unburden themselves of any stress felt during the process itself, ideally before going home. The outcome of the inspection is usually discussed in detail in a second meeting, once the inspection report has been received. At this stage, the setting will consider the actions staff should take in the light of the report's findings.

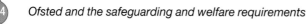

Index

imaginative, being
activity ideas   188,
191–96
ELG   191
information and records
260
about the child   262
about the provider
263–64
complaints   262–63
disclosure by
practitioners   248,
264
for parents and carers
262
sharing confidential
information   260–61
written policies   264–65
information, verbal and
non-verbal   51
injuries   256
inspections, Ofsted
being revised   266–72
coping with   272
grades   265
preparing for   266
procedure   266
results   265
instructions, use of   63
interest tables   71–72

J

jobs boards   107–08

K

key persons   37, 250–51
kinaesthetic learners
225–26

L

language *see*
communication and
language
learning and development
areas of   16, 22–25,
44–46
communication and   51
implementation of each
area   46–48

interconnection of areas
39
requirements   22–25,
44
tracking development
199–200
understanding
development   200–03
learning, effective   39–42,
48–49
learning styles   197–98,
225–27
library visits   136–37
listening and attention
activity ideas   54–60
ELG   54
literacy   23, 127
reading   128–37
roots of   127–28
writing   138–45
live performances and art
186–87
local authorities   28
locomotive movements   74
lotto   59–60, 228

M

mark-making skills   83,
138
mathematics   23, 145
numbers   146–53
shape, space and
measures   153–61
media and materials, using
activity ideas   183–91
ELG   183
medication
administering to children
254
staff taking   248–49
minor matters   268, 270
mobile phones, use of   245
morality   102
motor skills   73–75, 83
activities for   77, 79–82,
84–86, 88–89
movement, imaginative
188

moving and handling
activity ideas   76–89
ELG   76
music   55–56, 179, 188

N

names, children's own   134
narrative observation   208
National Literacy Trust   130
needs, understanding
children's   200
non-participant observers
214
numbers
activity ideas   146–53
ELG   146

O

object permanence   173
observation   205–06
assessing and evaluating
215–16
informing planning
216–17
methods of   207–13
with or without adults
213–15
Ofsted   30, 265
changes that must be
notified to   264
coping with inspection
272–74
inspections   265–66
revising regulation and
inspection   266–72

P

paperwork, limiting   204
parallel play   123
parents, working in
partnership with   197,
229–30, 239, 241, 261
Parten's five stages of play
123–24
participant observers   215
patterns   158
people and communities
activity ideas   162–72
ELG   162

Acknowledgements

The author and the publisher would also like to thank the following for permission to reproduce material.

Text permissions

There are references throughout to the following documents, as well as the Department for Education website, which are all Department of Education © Crown Copyright 2012:

- The Early Years: Foundations for life, health and learning, an independent report on the Early Years Foundation Stage to Her Majesty's Government (Dame Clare Tickell, 2011)

- Statutory Framework for the Early Years Foundation Stage (DfE, March 2012)

- Overall reforms to the 2012 EYFS framework (DfE, March 2012)

- Development Matters in the Early Years Foundation Stage (Early Education/DfE, March 2012)

- Regulation of providers on the Early Years Register: A report on the responses to consultation (Ofsted, May 2012)

All Crown Copyright material is reproduced under PSI licence no. C2009002012

pp 128–129 © National Literacy Trust 2012

pp 112–113 Copyright © 2012 – The Guild of Sensory Development

Photos

iStock: 1.1, 1.2, 1.4, 1.5, 1.6, 2.8, 2.2, 3.3, 3.9, 3.10, 3.14, 3.15, 3.16, 3.18, 3.20, 4.1, 4.2, 4.10, 4.15, 4.16, 5.1, 5.2, 5.3, 5.4, 5.5, 5.6, 5.7, 5.8, 5.9, 5.10, 5.11
Nicholas Yarsley/Wizzwam: 1.7, 3.12, 3.13, 3.17, 4.4, 4.18
www.heathergunnphotography.co.uk: 3.2, 3.5, 3.7, 3.11, 3.21, 3.22, 4.8
Martin Sookias: 3.7
Fotolia: 3.19

Every effort has been made to trace the copyright holders but if any have been inadvertently overlooked the publisher will be pleased to make the necessary arrangements at the first opportunity.